"Creative, insightful, experiential—this study has been designed with great care. It can take you deeper into the heart of a real pilgrimage with God."

— PAULA RINEHART, author of *Strong Women, Soft Hearts* and *What's He Really Thinking?*

A WOMAN'S
JOURNEY OF
DISCIPLESHIP

Friends ON THE JOURNEY

*Encouraging and
Equipping Women to
Disciple Others*

Gigi Busa

Ruth Fobes

Diane Manchester

NAVPRESS

*A NavPress resource published in alliance
with Tyndale House Publishers, Inc.*

NAVIGATOR **CHURCH** MINISTRIES

NAVPRESS

NavPress is the publishing ministry of The Navigators, an international Christian organization and leader in personal spiritual development. NavPress is committed to helping people grow spiritually and enjoy lives of meaning and hope through personal and group resources that are biblically rooted, culturally relevant, and highly practical.

For more information, visit www.NavPress.com.

The Navigators
P.O. Box 6000
Colorado Springs, CO 80934
www.navigatorchurchministries.org/ncm

CONTENTS

FROM THE HEARTS OF THE AUTHORS

A WOMAN'S JOURNEY OF DISCIPLESHIP was written by five women who have experienced firsthand the joy of discipleship and have longed to see God ignite this same passion in others. This three-book series is designed to launch women on their journeys with Jesus, capturing their hearts to follow Him and equipping them to disciple others.

A WOMAN'S JOURNEY OF DISCIPLESHIP is more than a Bible study series; it is a process through which women learn how to walk daily with the Lord and pass on to others that same discipling vision Jesus gave His disciples. Our prayer is that women's hearts everywhere would be ignited to follow Jesus Christ and in turn disciple others, leaving a legacy of spiritual generations. Our hearts are expressed in this verse:

We loved you so much that we were delighted to share with you not only the gospel of God but our lives as well, because you had become so dear to us.
(1 Thessalonians 2:8)

Will you join us on this great adventure?

ACKNOWLEDGMENTS

A WOMAN'S JOURNEY OF DISCIPLESHIP is sponsored by Navigator Church Ministries, a mission of The Navigators. Leadership training for this series is available. Visit The Navigators at www.navigatorchurchministries.org for more information. We thank God for those who contributed their ideas, expertise, and prayer throughout the writing process.

The authors are most grateful to Ron Bennett and John Purvis for their work on *The Adventure of Discipling Others*, which provided the foundational framework for the development of *Friends on the Journey*.

INTRODUCTION

The revelation of GOD is whole and pulls our lives together. The signposts of GOD are clear and point out the right road. The life-maps of GOD are right, showing the way to joy. The directions of God are plain and easy on the eyes.
(PSALM 19:7-8, MSG)

This third book in the series, *Friends on the Journey,* will lead you step by step in knowing how to equip others to grow in developing their relationship with Christ. *Friends* will provide opportunity to capture God's heart and vision for a life-long passion of discipling others. By investing your life in women within your sphere of influence you will experience the joy of seeing these women become captivated by this same vision. You are a precious link for future generations to know and love Jesus.

A WOMAN'S JOURNEY OF DISCIPLESHIP is laid out as a sequential process covered in three books: *Bridges on the Journey, Crossroads on the Journey,* and *Friends on the Journey.* However, each book stands alone and can be used separately.

Bridges on the Journey	introduces you	to your life in Christ
Crossroads on the Journey	invites you	to go deeper in your walk with Christ
Friends on the Journey	equips you	to invest your life in others

BRIDGES ON THE JOURNEY

God invites you into a relationship with Him. To begin this relationship, you must cross the bridge of trusting in Jesus and His salvation. After this initial step of faith, you will encounter other bridges that, as you cross them, will help establish your new relationship as God's child. *Bridges on the Journey* will help you form habits and attitudes that will result in intimacy with God, spiritual growth, and fruitfulness as you learn to follow Him daily.

CROSSROADS ON THE JOURNEY

The second book in the series invites you to take the next step on your journey. New steps often lead to a fork in the path: *Which way should I choose? Crossroads on the Journey* will help you use the Bible as your foremost resource for making daily life decisions. You will have opportunities to develop lifelong convictions to grow even deeper in your relationship with Christ and learn how to pass God's love on to others.

FRIENDS ON THE JOURNEY

Jesus taught His disciples by example, setting the pattern for His followers. Through your life and ministry, you can learn to encourage and equip others, who will in turn invest their lives in future generations. This final book in the series is intended to empower you with God's vision and passion and give you the skills for a lifelong ministry of discipling others.

WHAT TO EXPECT IN *FRIENDS ON THE JOURNEY*

Friends on the Journey seeks to establish in women God's vision and passion for lifelong discipling of others, who in turn will invest their lives in future generations. It will help you to answer important questions such as these:

- What are your hopes and dreams for your journey with Jesus?
- Who will follow you?
- What spiritual legacy will you leave for the next generation?

Friends on the Journey has been used successfully to develop leaders who have caught the vision of discipling others. It is intended for women who have already established their relationship with Christ and are ready to disciple others.

Friends on the Journey is an excellent resource for leadership development. It provides:

- Vision and tools for training in outreach and discipleship focused at impacting future generations for Christ
- Bible studies that develop character and spiritual maturity
- Opportunities to grow in spiritual habits aimed at personal commitment and a lifetime of following God

Friends on the Journey includes the following components:

- **My Daily Journey** is a record, written in your own journal, of your daily discoveries about God and yourself and what God has been saying to you each day.
- **Our Journey Together** is a time for group members to share recent highlights from their devotional journals along with lessons learned on their journeys.
- **Reflections from the Heart of a Discipler** are women's personal stories that will reveal God's vision for discipling others.
- **The Travel Guide** leads you to a deeper understanding as you explore and experience what the Bible says about your life.
- **Writings Along the Way** gives additional perspective from other travelers on their spiritual journeys.
- **Tips for the Road** is a section that offers practical help and encouragement on your journey of discipleship.
- **Learning the Route by Heart** invites you to memorize God's Word systematically and allow it to change your life. Bookmarks with each week's memory verses are provided toward the end of the book. Through consistent review of the verses, you will strengthen the vital habit of Scripture memorization.
- **Next Steps on the Journey** gives the assignment to be completed before the next meeting.
- **My Journey Friends** is a record of your fellow group members' names, phone numbers, and e-mail addresses to help you keep in touch with one another. Please take the time during your first meeting to write down this information in appendix A.

THE DISCIPLING VISION

"AM I WILLING TO CARRY THE TORCH?"

*He said to his disciples, "The harvest is plentiful but the workers
are few. Ask the Lord of the harvest, therefore, to send out workers
into his harvest field."*
(MATTHEW 9:37-38)

Often when we are about our own business, God interrupts us to share His heart
and give us a bigger vision for our journey with Him. Vision is related not to
what we want but to what is on God's heart. Repeatedly in His Word, we see God
using ordinary men and women to impact the people of their generation in extraordinary ways.

If you could look down from heaven at the panoramic vision God has for the
world, you would see that the gospel was carried forward by the faithful and obedient,
from one generation to the next. Then by saying yes to the gospel and allowing Jesus
to reign in your heart, you have the privilege of obeying God's command to disciple
and to intentionally invest in the women around you on this journey of discipleship.
You are the link for future generations to know and love Jesus Christ!

We invite you to explore the heart of disciplemaking, the harvest promised by
Jesus, and your part in leaving a legacy for spiritual generations to come.

MY DAILY JOURNEY

The first two books of this series included a daily devotional guide called My Daily Journey. In the first book, readers looked at the gospel of Mark; in the second, the gospel of John. In *Friends on the Journey*, you will turn your focus to the acts of the Holy Spirit. The kingdom of God spread from person to person as God empowered each one to share the gospel of Jesus and equip these new believers.

Rather than provide a daily guide for *Friends on the Journey*, we encourage you to develop your own daily reading plan for the book of Acts and write your thoughts in your personal journal. This practice will help you establish the joy of a lifetime habit of meeting with the Lord.

As you read and journal your thoughts, you will come to know God better and more clearly understand that His plans for the world involve your participation. You can take your part in the movement of the Holy Spirit as God's kingdom continues to spread one woman at a time! Use these questions to guide you:

- What did I learn about God or myself on my journey?
- How can I grow deeper in my relationship with the Lord or demonstrate His love to others?

This is our conversation with God: He speaks to us from His Word, and we respond to Him in prayer.

In your journal, write out thoughts from your devotional times: what you are learning about God or yourself, how these truths can help you grow deeper in relationship with Him, and how you can demonstrate His love to others.

OUR JOURNEY TOGETHER

In your group:

- Write the names of your group members on the My Journey Friends pages (see appendix A).
- Taking turns, read the introduction to this book aloud (pages 9–11).

- Share a recent highlight from your personal devotional times.
- Express any inadequacies you may feel as you think about discipling others.
- Share with the group names of women God may be bringing to your mind as people He may want you to disciple.
- Review together your memory verse, Matthew 9:37-38.

Reflections from the Heart of a Discipler
"Life-Changing Friendships on the Journey," by Gigi Busa

When I was a young mom, a friend opened up my dusty Bible and showed me that what Jesus had done on the cross two thousand years earlier was for *me*. Until that time, I hadn't understood that heaven was a promise from God, guaranteed by His Son's death. It took me two years to accept that eternal life was so simple and to invite Jesus into my life.

I soon discovered, however, that although receiving Christ was simple, living His new way of life was not! Much of my spiritual foundation had been tradition, religion, and misguided thinking. I realized that I needed to know more of the Bible so I would not miss anything God had for me. I joined a Bible study led by a woman named Elaine who deeply loved God and knew His Word. Whenever group members asked her a question, she would direct us to the Word and often would quote it. It was obvious to me that the Bible shaped Elaine's life and relationships. I asked her, "I've met many Christian women, but your love for Jesus stands out to me. Why?" In response, Elaine told me about discipleship, which she described as one person helping another grow in the Lord, allowing the Scriptures and the Holy Spirit to change that person's life. Many years before, a friend, Chris, had discipled her. I realized that a discipling relationship like that was exactly what I needed and wanted. I blurted out, "Will you disciple me?" Little did I know that for years Elaine had been praying someone would ask her that specific question.

Elaine and I began meeting together, using discipleship books by The Navigators. It was not just studying the books that radically changed my life, however. It was also the experience of having another woman sit with me and open her life and heart to me. Elaine lived out 1 Thessalonians 2:7-8: *"We proved to be gentle among you, as a nursing mother tenderly cares for her own children. We loved you so much that we were delighted to share with you not only the gospel of God but also our own lives"* (NASB, NIV).

Elaine's authenticity and vulnerability about her personal challenges and sin created an atmosphere where I could candidly share my struggles. Elaine listened and did not try to fix me. She continually encouraged me to look to the Bible and trust the Lord. She taught me how to have daily times with Jesus in His Word and how to apply the Scriptures to my life.

Elaine's love for Jesus and His Word was contagious. Before long, I had caught her passion; my excitement about Jesus became so uncontainable that others started to notice changes in me. I asked Elaine to disciple my friends also but was disappointed to hear her say she did not have time to teach them.

"Who will teach them if you don't?" I asked.

"You will," she replied.

Figuring that she might not have noticed, I relayed my lack of credentials: "I have been meeting with you for only two months. I don't know much at all. What if they ask me something I don't know?"

"You are not growing because of what I know," Elaine assured me, "but because of Who I know." Although she continued to meet with me, Elaine lovingly moved me out of the "nursery" and helped me begin to teach others.

Clearly I was discipling women not because I thought I was capable but because I wanted them to have the opportunity to know Jesus the same way I knew Him, I trusted the Lord to help me. Through the experience of seeing Him use me, a young Christian, to teach another, I discovered that my heart's passion was discipleship. I loved teaching others to love Jesus and obey His Word.

My life was like a pebble thrown into the middle of a pond, making one ripple upon another ripple until the ripples met the shore. One life lived for the Lord and invested in another could have impact for generations to come! Jesus had given the Great Commission: to go and make disciples of all nations. The twelve people Jesus discipled went on to disciple others who in turn discipled still others. Now I, too, was part of His Commission, and as time went on, the women I discipled also went on to disciple others.

Behind us are many people who have given their lives so others would know Jesus Christ. Before us is the challenge to keep discipleship going from generation to generation. This is the discipling vision. Go and make disciples. Look — don't you see it? The fields are ripe for harvest!

THE TRAVEL GUIDE

Can you identify with Gigi's initial feelings of inadequacy and fear at the thought of discipling someone? As you will see in this section's Scripture passages, believers find courage and boldness to disciple others based on God's Word, Jesus' example, and their God-given passion to reach out with the gospel. But it is always the power of God's Holy Spirit that changes people.

1. Read and reflect on Matthew 9:35-38 and respond to the following questions.

   a. What did Jesus see in the people around Him? How did He respond to them (see verses 35-36)?

   b. What dilemma does Jesus lay before us (see verses 37-38)?

   c. What does He command us to do?

2. *The Message* paraphrase of Matthew 9:38 says, *"On your knees and pray for harvest hands!"* Write a short prayer expressing to God your heart for the harvest.

3. Read 1 Corinthians 3:5-11.

   a. What were the roles of Apollos and Paul in the harvest? What do you think their unique responsibilities might have been in this work they did together with God?

   b. What rewards does God offer to us in this harvest (see verses 8-9)?

   c. What are your gut feelings about your own involvement and responsibilities in expanding God's kingdom?

d. What in this passage encourages you?

4. Spiritual generations are similar to family generations. Think of family traditions that have been handed down to you that you would like to pass on. Why is keeping certain traditions alive in future generations important to you? What life lessons has God taught you that you would want to pass on to others?

5. Read Psalm 78:1-8 and Deuteronomy 6:6-9.

   a. Psalm 78 describes a perpetuation of both physical and spiritual generations. According to this passage, in what ways are God's people called to cultivate spiritual generations?

   b. What happens when God's life-giving words are passed on?

c. How can you convey God's vision of discipling others in your day-to-day activities while "walking along the road"? Give specific examples.

Earlier we saw Paul's ultimate vision of the God who calls you into His own kingdom and glory (see 1 Thessalonians 2:12). Now we have looked at the breadth of God's vision: the bountiful harvest of bringing people into His kingdom. We also have looked at the depth of telescopic vision of generations — biological and spiritual — of people coming into His kingdom, and we are one of the links in this chain.

6. Read 2 Timothy 2:2 and Revelation 7:9-10 and think about spiritual generations.

   a. According to 2 Timothy 2, who witnessed to and discipled Timothy?

   b. Who did Timothy in turn witness to and disciple (see 1 Corinthians 4:17; Philippians 2:22; 1 Thessalonians 3:2; 1 Timothy 1:3)?

c. Use your imagination to picture the scene described in Revelation 7:9-10. Do you think some of the people in that huge crowd of worshippers could be there because of Paul's vision expressed in 2 Timothy 2:2? How many? How many could be there if you were to pass on the gospel as Paul and Timothy did?

7. Who would you like to see come to Christ over the next few years? What role could you have in reaching out to them and building deeply into their lives? Dream big! No dream is too wild because everything is possible with God. Write down the list of people you dreamed about just now, and add their names to your prayer list. Now read Ephesians 3:20. How does this verse encourage you to pray boldly?

8. 1 Thessalonians 2:7-12 describes Paul's relationship with new believers.

   a. Using key words and phrases, how does Paul convey his heart toward those he discipled?

b. What message is strongly linked to his warm relationship with the people he discipled (see verse 8)?

c. In verse 12 Paul casts an ultimate vision for the people he ministers to. In your own words, describe that vision.

d. How would you feel if you could have a relationship like the one described in this passage? If you have had such a relationship, what were some of the highlights and encouragement you experienced in it?

9. Read 1 Corinthians 4:14-17 and 1 Thessalonians 1:6-7, paying special attention to the repeated words *imitate* and *model*.

a. What are some character qualities of people who have influenced your spiritual journey?

b. As you picture yourself reaching out to other women, what character qualities would you want to model for them?

In the Bible, God gives us portraits of real people with real misgivings about their own abilities to carry out the ministry to which God calls them.

10. Read Jeremiah 1:6; 1 Timothy 4:12, Exodus 3:1-14; 4:1-31.

a. What reason did Jeremiah give for not wanting to speak on God's behalf? What did Paul say to Timothy, who apparently had similar reservations?

b. In Exodus 3:4-14, what was God's vision for the nation of Israel and for Moses' part in that?

c. According to Exodus 3 and 4, what were Moses' objections to God's call? How do you think he felt about what God was asking of him?

d. From Exodus 3:12, 14 and 4:11, what answers were given to allay Moses' concerns? Which ones apply to *your* concerns about what God may be calling you to do?

e. Despite his feelings, Moses chose to trust God. What was the "ripple effect" of his obedient actions (see Exodus 4:28-31)?

11. Use Ephesians 3:20 as the basis for a prayer that shares with God your willingness to rely on Him for what you need to reach out to others: *"God who by his mighty power at work within us is able to do far more than we would ever dare to ask or even dream of—infinitely beyond our highest prayers, desires, thoughts, or hopes"* (TLB).

a. What assurances does God give in this passage?

b. How do the passages you just read dispel your perceived inadequacies and motivate you in discipling others?

God's adequacy is seen *after* we step out in obedience to His call.

> A God big enough to make you afraid is powerful enough
> to accomplish all He is about to ask of you.
> — Calvin Miller, *The Christ of Christmas*

WRITINGS ALONG THE WAY

A Heart for People

by Lee Brase[1]

A disciplemaker must love those he wants to help. In addition, love sees people the way they are and then serves them.

A disciplemaker's goal is to build people up in Christ. It was Paul's love, more than his knowledge and abilities, that established hundreds of Christians throughout Asia Minor and Europe. He was able to write to the Thessalonians, *"As apostles of Christ we could have been a burden to you, but we were gentle among you, like a mother caring for her little children. We loved you so much that we were delighted to share with you not only the gospel of God but our lives as well, because you had become so dear to us"* (1 Thessalonians 2:6-8).

Love, like faith, expresses itself in action. That's why Paul went on to say to the Thessalonians, *"Surely you remember, brothers, our toil and hardship; we worked night and day in order not to be a burden to anyone while we preached the gospel of God to you"* (1 Thessalonians 2:9). Serving is love in action.

This liberated me from thinking of discipling as getting people through programs and methods. I began thinking of how to serve each person to help him become more mature in Christ. The person, not my program, became the focus.

Every human being has needs and burdens. They're necessary for growth. We help people grow when we "carry each other's burdens" (Galatians 6:2). Doing this takes a servant's heart.

We have a beautiful picture of serving in Jesus' life. *"Come to me, all you who are weary and burdened, and I will give you rest"* (Matthew 11:28). His invitation came at the end of a very difficult day. Jesus had just had to denounce the cities in which most of His miracles had been performed because the people didn't repent (Matthew 11:20). People who questioned His motives had called Him a glutton and a drunkard

(Matthew 11:19). John the Baptist had just sent some of his disciples to ask Jesus, *"Are you the one who was to come, or should we expect someone else?"* (Matthew 11:2-3).

Jesus had had enough disappointments that day to make most of us withdraw, sulk, and cry.

However, He invited others to bring their cares and burdens to Him.

Love gives us the capacity to serve others even when our burdens are heavy. It enables us to put our cares aside for the moment and give ourselves to someone else. Without love, we'll never truly disciple others. They'll have to fit into our schedule and needs — and they won't, and shouldn't have to.

 TIPS FOR THE ROAD

Prayer is a vital part of preparing our hearts and lives to be used by God. We should also pray that the Holy Spirit will prepare other women's hearts to hear God's message. No matter how eloquent our words may be, only God can change a person's heart. Here's a practical suggestion to help you get in the habit of praying regularly for the women you'd like to influence for Christ.

- From your list of women, ask God which three He'd like you to focus on over the next season of your life.
- Write these three names on an index card and put it in your Bible where you will see it every day.
- Pray daily for these women. In your prayers, remember to ask the Lord to give you opportunities to share with these women about your love for Him and His love for them.

LEARNING THE ROUTE BY HEART

When we travel often to the same destination, there comes a time when we no longer need a map. That's because we've memorized the route by heart. It is similar in our spiritual journeys. When we have God's Word stored in our hearts, it serves as a map to get us through life's challenges and safely to our destination. There are many benefits to memorizing the Scriptures.

Psalm 119:11 says that Scripture keeps us from sin, which is helpful if we want to be like Jesus: "I have hidden your word in my heart that I might not sin against you." Psalm 119:105 says that Scripture gives us guidance and direction for our lives: "Your word is a lamp to my feet and a light for my path."

Use the tear-out bookmarks provided in appendix C to help you memorize each week's primary verse. Keep the verse with you as you go through your day so you can review it often. Look at it again before you sleep. As you continually keep God's Word in front of you, He will begin to infuse your heart with His wisdom.

The Great Commission reveals God's heart and vision for your life journey. As you memorize your verse for the next session, think about the privilege you have of intentionally investing in other women's lives.

Topic: The Great Commission

Then Jesus came to them and said, "All authority in heaven and on earth has been given to me. Therefore go and make disciples of all nations, baptizing them in the name of the Father and of the Son and of the Holy Spirit, and teaching them to obey everything I have commanded you. And surely I am with you always, to the very end of the age."

(MATTHEW 28:18-20)

Next Steps on the Journey

Complete these items before the next meeting:
- Read and complete "Session 2: The Great Commission."
- Memorize Matthew 28:18-20 and review Matthew 9:37-38.
- Read Acts 1-4 and come prepared to share a recent devotional highlight from your journal.
- Pray daily for your three women.

THE GREAT COMMISSION

"How can I develop God's passion for the world?"

*Jesus came to them and said, "All authority in heaven and
on earth has been given to me. Therefore go and make disciples of
all nations, baptizing them in the name of the Father and of the
Son and of the Holy Spirit, and teaching them to obey everything I
have commanded you. And surely I am with you always,
to the very end of the age."*
(MATTHEW 28:18-20)

You are beginning to understand God's panoramic vision for spiritual generations and how He can enable you when you feel inadequate in reaching out to disciple others. In this session, you will begin to see a huge part of God's heart — the Great Commission — and understand even more how developing a passion for God's vision for making disciples can change the way you relate to others.

We invite you to hear Jesus' words and discover your role in the Great Commission.

MY DAILY JOURNEY

In your journal, write out thoughts from your devotional times: what you are learning about God or yourself, how these truths can help you grow deeper in relationship with Him, and how you can demonstrate His love to others.

OUR JOURNEY TOGETHER

In your group:

- Talk about a recent highlight from your personal devotional times. What has God been saying to you?
- Review together your memory verse, Matthew 28:18-20.
- Share how praying daily for your three women has affected you.

Reflections from the Heart of a Discipler

"A World-Reaching Vision," by Ruth Fobes

Like many eighteen-year-olds, as high school graduation drew near, I spent a lot of time pondering my future: *What should I do with my life? Where will I live? Who will I marry?* Then, all of a sudden, my world came crashing down on me: A friend my age died! I was shocked and afraid. *How could anyone so young die, just like that?*

For days this tragedy consumed me. I reflected on my friend's life and what it meant. I tried to process by writing poems about him. He was an example to me of someone who had wholeheartedly followed Jesus. For the first time in my life, I wondered what it really meant to follow Christ.

At my friend's funeral, the pastor said something that captured my heart. "Sometimes God allows things like this to happen even if it's just to help one person," said Pastor Jim. I whispered, "That's me." I felt my soul stirring within me in a way I'd never before experienced. In that moment, I knew my life was going to change.

Later that day, Pastor Jim's family invited me to attend a Christian concert with them. That evening, the words of one of the songs pierced my heart. Right there in my seat, I had a conversation with God. "Lord, I want to give my life completely to You. I'm going to pursue a life of learning what it means to walk with You."

Days before my high school graduation, I met with Pastor Jim to discuss my future. He affirmed me and encouraged me to pursue attending a Christian college and spoke blessings over my life. I felt as though he had symbolically put a crown over me for me to grow into and that God had guided him in directing my future.

College meant a whole new world of things for which to trust God, and on my new path of journeying with Jesus, I determined to grasp any learning opportunities I could. But at the same time, an eager anticipation swelled up inside me. The Lord would be with me. He would show me the way just as Pastor Jim had said.

And He did! The moment I began my journey of wholeheartedly following Christ, I experienced miraculous answers to prayer and felt His presence every step of the way. God offered me many opportunities to grow, including the chance to be discipled by a woman named Millie. She helped me discover promises from the Bible that I could stake my life on. She ignited my vision to pursue a life of discipling others. She taught me to turn the verses I memorized into prayers.

I was amazed and thrilled at how God answered my prayers. I began to converse with the Lord whenever and wherever. I felt blessed to have had someone take such an interest in helping me pursue a life of following the Lord and His will for me.

But God was doing something bigger in me: He was igniting my heart with the truth that He loved all the people in the entire world just as much as He loved me. And because He loved others that much, He wanted me to share this big-picture vision too. My passion grew as I spent time listening to the Lord through daily times in His Word and through prayer, so passionate that I wrote a song called "A Vision for the World."

For me, God's vision meant being able to see people come to Christ, develop a heart for God, grow in their faith, become disciples of Christ, and reproduce this vision in others. This vision lined up with Jesus' Great Commission from Matthew 28:18-20. During that pivotal season in my life, I began to pursue that vision with my entire body, soul, and spirit. Years later, I can honestly say that nothing could be more thrilling to me. Jesus called me to follow Him in pursuing a world-reaching vision. He invites you also to choose this path.

_____

THE TRAVEL GUIDE

You have seen how the Great Commission was influential in Ruth's response to God's call on her life. Now look more closely at the Great Commission and how it can change *your* life and allow God's love to flow through you into the lives of people around you. You will also look at the Great Commandment and see how it influences and shapes your call to share Jesus with others.

The Great Commission

Jesus gave His apprentices some important parting words before He returned to heaven. *The Message* puts it this way: *"Jesus, undeterred, went right ahead and gave his charge: 'God authorized and commanded me to commission you: Go out and train everyone you meet, far and near, in this way of life, marking them by baptism in the three-fold name: Father, Son, and Holy Spirit. Then instruct them in the practice of all I have commanded you. I'll be with you as you do this, day after day after day, right up to the end of the age'"* (Matthew 28:18-20).

1. Using the table on the next page, record your observations regarding the different gospel expressions of the Great Commission.

READ THE SCRIPTURES	WHAT ARE THE COMMAND/ACTION VERBS?	WHAT ARE THE KEY IDEAS/MAJOR EMPHASES?	WHAT IS OUR SOURCE OF POWER FOR DISCIPLING OTHERS?
Matthew 28:18-20			
Mark 16:15-20			
Luke 24:44-49			
John 20:19-23; 21:5-6,15-19			

a. What ideas are common to each of these passages?

b. What specific instructions do these passages give regarding communicating the gospel?

2. Read Matthew 28:18-20 again.

a. What are the implications regarding the authority Jesus has been given?

b. How would you explain the meaning of "go" in these verses?

c. Jesus calls all of us to "make disciples." What do you think is involved in making disciples? How could making disciples become your personal call?

d. "[Teach] them to obey everything I have commanded you" (verse 20) is a powerful statement. As a disciple of Jesus Christ, how could you be obedient to His command?

3. Reflect on the passages you studied in the chart on page 35 and write a summary of the Great Commission as you understand it.

4. Using your summary as a foundation, write a prayer in response to Jesus' Great Commission, picturing how you would live out His call and asking Him to help you.

The gospel is the heart and the vision of God for the world, and in His grace He has entrusted us with this precious message.

5. Read 1 Thessalonians 2:4 and 2 Timothy 1:14.

a. How would you define the word *entrusted*?

b. According to the passages you just read, what are the implications of being entrusted with the gospel?

c. What do these verses say about what God has entrusted to us?

6. In view of what God has entrusted to you personally, how can you begin to influence the people you are praying for?

7. In her story, Ruth said she pursued the vision God had given her with her entire body, soul, and spirit. What might hinder you from living out that kind of commitment?

Ask God to help you overcome these hindrances.

8. How would your priorities and schedule change if you were to make the Great Commission an integral part of your life?

> *He is no fool who gives what he cannot keep*
> *to gain that which he cannot lose.*
> —missionary Jim Elliot, *from his journal, October 28, 1949*

The Great Commandment

9. Compare the Great Commission (see Matthew 28:18-20) with the Great Commandment (see Matthew 22:37-39). How could you express the Great Commandment as you live out the Great Commission? Why is it so important to do so? Give specific, practical examples of how these two mandates might work together as you reach out to the women you are praying for and hoping to disciple.

The Great Commandment pulls us together in fellowship with one another while following the Great Commission can take us apart.

WRITINGS ALONG THE WAY

Born to Reproduce

by Dawson E. Trotman[1]

A few years ago, while visiting Edinburgh, Scotland, I stood on High Street just down from the castle. As I stood there, I saw a father and a mother coming toward me pushing a baby carriage. They looked very happy, were well dressed, and apparently were well to do.

I watched them for a little while as they walked on and thought how beautiful it is that God permits a man to choose one woman who seems the most beautiful and lovely to him, and she chooses him out of all the men whom she has ever known. Then they separate themselves to one another, and God in His plan gives them the means of reproduction! It is a wonderful thing that a little child should be born into their family, having some of the father's characteristics and some of the mother's, some of his looks and some of hers.

As I continued to stand there I saw another baby carriage coming in my direction. It was a secondhand affair and very wobbly. Obviously, the father and mother were poor. Both were dressed poorly and plainly, but when I indicated my interest in seeing their baby, they stopped and with the same pride as the other parents let me view their little pink-cheeked, beautiful-eyed child.

I thought as these went on their way, "God gave this little baby whose parents are poor everything that He gave the other. It has five little fingers on each hand, a little mouth, and two eyes. Properly cared for, those little hands may someday be the hands of an artist or a musician."

Then this other thought came to me, "Isn't it wonderful that God did not select the wealthy and the educated and say, 'You can have children,' and to the poor and the uneducated say, 'You cannot.' Everyone on earth has that privilege."

The first order ever given to man was that he "be fruitful and multiply." In other words, he was to reproduce after his own kind. "Multiply. I want more just like you, more in My own image."

Twenty-three years ago we took a born-again sailor and spent some time with him, showing him how to reproduce spiritually after his kind. It took time, lots of time. We took care of his problems and taught him not only to hear God's Word and to read it but also how to study it. We taught him how to fill the quiver of his heart with the arrows of God's Word so that the Spirit of God could lift an arrow from his heart and place it to the bow of his lips and pierce a heart for Christ.

He found a number of men on his ship, but none of them would go all out for the Lord. He came to me after a month of this and said, "Dawson, I can't get any of these guys on the ship to get down to business."

I said to him, "Listen, ask God to give you one. You can't have two until you have one. Ask God to give you a man after your own heart."

He began to pray. One day he came to me and said, "I think I've found him." Later he brought the young fellow over. Three months from the time that I started to work with him, he had found a man of like heart. He worked with this new babe in Christ, and those two fellows began to grow and spiritually reproduce. On that ship 125 men found the Savior before it was sunk at Pearl Harbor. Men off that first battleship are in four continents of the world as missionaries today.

You can lead a soul to Christ from twenty minutes to a couple of hours. But it takes from twenty weeks to a couple of years to get him on the road to maturity, victorious over the sins and the recurring problems that come along. He must learn how to make right decisions.

Where is your man? Where is your woman? Do you have one? You can ask God for one.

 **TIPS FOR THE ROAD**

Invite one of the women on your prayer list to lunch or coffee to begin developing or deepening your relationship. Ask God to help you create a safe environment for her.

A safe atmosphere is fostered by your own example of honesty, humility, and transparency. Your friend must feel that she can freely express herself without correction or shame and that you will understand her. Accept your friend where she actually is without pushing her to be where you think she should be. Remember, your first purpose is to develop a friendship.

As your friendship grows, ask God to give you opportunities for spiritual openings. It may take several conversations before your friend feels safe enough to open up to you. When you sense she is comfortable with you and knows you care about her, ask God to give you some good open-ended questions to ask that will help you know her better. Open-ended questions include such words as *how*, *what*, and *who* and cannot be answered simply *yes* or *no*. For instance, He might lead you to ask:

- What has your spiritual journey been so far?
- Who has been especially influential in your life?
- Have you ever experienced a personal relationship with Jesus? When? How did your relationship begin?

You can follow up on your friend's response with, "I'd like to hear more about that." Or if you discover that your friend is already a believer and growing in Christ, you might try asking, "What have you learned about God or yourself while reading the Bible this week?"

The best questions come from genuine communication that shows you have been listening and you care. If you look at Jesus' conversations, you will see that He often used questions that led people in a process of personal exploration rather than telling them what to think. For instance, in Matthew 16:13, Jesus asked the disciples a question to help them understand who he was: "Who do people say the Son of Man is?" When the disciples responded with what they thought others would say, Jesus followed up with a more penetrating second question: "But what about you? Who do you say I am?"

Get together with two or three other women sometime and brainstorm some questions that encourage spiritual conversations below the surface details.

LEARNING THE ROUTE BY HEART

Ministering life-to-life means embracing God's heart and vision to link you in personal relationship with other women. As you memorize 1 Thessalonians 2:7-8 for the next session, think about how you can have an effective relationship with the women you disciple.

Topic: Ministering Life-to-Life

We were gentle among you, like a mother caring for her little children. We loved you so much that we were delighted to share with you not only the gospel of God but our lives as well, because you had become so dear to us.

(1 THESSALONIANS 2:7-8)

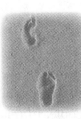

Next Steps on the Journey

Complete these items before the next meeting:

- Read and complete "Session 3: Friends on the Journey."
- Memorize 1 Thessalonians 2:7-8 and review the verses from previous sessions.
- Read Acts 5-7 and come prepared to share a recent devotional highlight from your journal.
- Share how you reached out to one of your friends whom you are praying to disciple. Pray for this developing friendship.

FRIENDS ON THE JOURNEY

"What does it mean to minister life-to-life?"

*We were gentle among you, like a mother caring for her
little children. We loved you so much that we were delighted to
share with you not only the gospel of God but our lives as well,
because you had become so dear to us.*

(1 Thessalonians 2:7-8)

By now you are not only starting to understand the *command* of Christ to *make* disciples but also seeing the special "loving trust" that God has given to you. Disciplemaking requires a love relationship with God and with other people. In this session, you will look at the discipling relationship and discover how you can experience an effective life-to-life ministry.

We invite you to embrace God's heart and vision for linking you with other women in personal, effective discipling relationships.

MY DAILY JOURNEY

In your journal, write out thoughts from your devotional times: what you are learning about God and yourself, how these truths can help you grow deeper in relationship with Him, and how you can demonstrate His love to others.

OUR JOURNEY TOGETHER

In your group:

- Share a recent highlight from your personal devotional times.
- Review together your memory verse, 1 Thessalonians 2:7-8.
- Discuss thoughts God gave you about bridging the gap between friendship and discipleship as you prayed for a woman you are befriending.
- Share concerns that have come to mind as you have begun this discipleship journey.

Reflections from the Heart of a Discipler

"Mentoring Toward Maturity," by Lynn Austin[1]

"I don't know what to do," my neighbor Gail sobbed over the phone. "Will you please pray for me?" I grabbed my Bible and hurried next door. Gail was a fairly new Christian who relied heavily on me to give advice, answer questions, and pray for her. "God is so good to give me a neighbor who's a mature Christian," she often said.

I enjoyed feeling needed by Gail and returned home each time satisfied that God had used me. But it bothered me that after so much time, Gail hadn't seemed to grow any stronger as a Christian. Hebrews 5:12 seemed to describe her: "Though by this time you ought to be teachers, you need someone to teach you the elementary truths of God's word all over again. You need milk, not solid food!" Something seemed to be wrong, but I didn't know what.

At the elementary school where I taught, I was studying mentoring. The concept was that experienced teachers were to team up with beginners to ease their transition into teaching. I learned that the goal of mentoring was to lead the beginner through a process of growth from dependence to independence. In order to reach the goal of independence, the mentoring relationship would need to change gradually and intentionally as the mentor progressed through a series of five roles: teacher, coach, collaborator, sponsor, and counselor.

With the mentoring process in mind, I thought of Gail. That's what's wrong, I realized. Gail's not growing in her Christian walk because my role with her has never changed. I enjoy being needed, and I've kept her dependent on me, stunting her spiritual growth. I was seeing that God desired for Gail to "leave the elementary teachings about Christ and go on to maturity" (Hebrews 6:1).

That same year, God sent Donna into my life and we became good friends. When she accepted Christ, I wanted to help her grow in faith and attain a vital, living relationship with God. I decided to apply the principles I'd learned and see if I could become Donna's mentor.

A Teacher

The mentor's first role is that of a teacher: giving instructions, explanations, and guidance. At this stage, the mentor intentionally models a process and the beginner observes and asks questions.

I answered many questions as Donna and I spent time together almost daily. I told her how to know for sure that she was born again, showed her how to find passages in the Bible, advised her about decisions she had to make, and prayed aloud for her. But most important, I tried to live my Christian life well because I knew my example was teaching Donna as much as my words were.

A Coach

The second role a mentor fulfills is that of a coach. She still leads, but it's time for the disciple to get into the game. The responsibility for growth begins to shift. At this stage, the mentor says, "Now you do it and I'll observe."

Donna joined the women's Bible study I led. As we proceeded through the lessons, I became her coach, standing back to watch and cheer as Donna acted. She soon grew confident in her ability to read the Scriptures and began contributing more to the discussions. Instead of answering all her questions, I showed Donna where to look in the Bible and encouraged her to read it herself. Instead of telling her what to do, I explained God's principles, encouraged her to ask God for guidance, and then helped her decide. We began to pray together.

A Collaborator

Gradually, the mentor's role shifts to that of a collaborator. Now the two people share responsibility for growth equally. They resolve questions and problems together in a give-and-take relationship, with the mentor's experience serving as a safeguard against the beginner's mistakes.

I watched Donna's faith grow quickly as God worked in her life. More and more, I encouraged Donna to go directly to God for answers to her questions or for guidance and direction in her life. I served as a collaborator, sounding board, and safety net, and she grew in confidence as I affirmed her decisions. Donna had become more independent of me and more dependent upon God.

A Sponsor

In the field of education, the mentor's role changes to sponsor when she introduces the beginner to the broader professional community, giving her opportunity to network with others and exposing her to additional resources, such as organizations and seminars. The mentor also serves as an advocate, recommending the newcomer for positions of responsibility. Similarly, in spiritual mentoring, an expert sponsor will notice suitable positions of spiritual service and responsibility when they open up and recommend the disciple for them.

Donna's enthusiastic, take-charge personality merged well with her deep spiritual hunger. Soon she began reaching out to others. In my role as sponsor, I led Donna to the resources she needed to deepen her spiritual walk and help others. The responsibility for her spiritual growth was almost entirely hers; I merely provided a nudge from time to time.

A Counselor

The mentor's final role is that of a counselor. In this stage, the disciple functions independently, while the mentor advises and provides perspective. The apprenticeship is nearly complete. The disciple now assumes full responsibility for her continued growth, but the mentor remains available to serve as a counselor and friend.

As time passed, Donna became very active in the church we both attended. When she learned that our annual women's retreat might be canceled due to lack of leadership, she volunteered to serve as chairwoman.

I felt satisfied that I'd done more for Donna than provide crisis intervention and a shoulder to lean on. In my role as mentor, I'd helped prepare her *"for works of service, so that the body of Christ may be built up"* (Ephesians 4:12). We'd reached the final goal of discipleship: Rather than being dependent on me, her mentor, Donna was dependent on the Lord.

A Mature Christian

During this time, Gail also grew in her relationship with the Lord. As a mother bird does, I gently pushed Gail out of her comfortable nest. Gradually, she became more dependent on God and less dependent on me.

STAGE	DEFINITION	POSSIBLE ACTIVITIES	RELATIONSHIPS
TEACHER	Mentor models a process and gives direct help; disciple observes and asks questions	Demonstrate how to read Scripture; pray aloud for disciple; model Christian lifestyle	Disciple is dependent on mentor
COACH	Mentor observes and directs as disciple practices new tasks	Encourage Bible study; pray with disciple; help disciple make decisions based on biblical principle	Disciple is 25 percent independent of mentor
COLLABORATOR	Mentor and disciple work together cooperatively in give-and-take relationship	Discuss Scripture together; encourage a prayer journal; encourage disciple to seek God's direction	Disciple is 50 percent independent of mentor
SPONSOR	Mentor introduces disciple to resources and wider network; mentor sponsors disciple for areas of ministry	Recommend books, organizations, and seminars for independent study; help disciple find and use gifts in ministry	Disciple is 75 percent independent of mentor
COUNSELOR	Disciple functions independently; mentor advises and provides perspective	Help set long-range spiritual goals; advise disciple as she mentors others	Disciple is independent of mentor

Another way to look at the transition of the "disciplemaker decreasing and the disciple increasing" is in this graph:

DISCIPLEMAKER

DISCIPLE

Teacher   **Coach**   **Collaborator**   **Sponsor**   **Counselor**

As you can see, the disciplemaker changes roles from being "sage on the stage" to "guide on the side"!

THE TRAVEL GUIDE

Disciplemaking is a relational ministry of one person helping another become mature in Christ. By life-to-life we mean the relational concept of one life personally touching another. Life-to-life ministry goes beyond transferring concepts or principles; a life-to-life relationship involves intentionally passing on values, heart, vision, passion, knowledge, and skills. Life-to-life relationships can be one-to-one or in the small-group context.

> *I no longer call you servants, because a servant does not know his master's business. Instead, I have called you friends, for everything that I learned from my Father I have made known to you. You did not choose me, but I chose you and appointed you to go and bear fruit—fruit that will last. Then the Father will give you whatever you ask in my name. This is my command: Love each other.* (John 15:15-17)

1. According to this passage, what does "I chose you" say about God's heart?

Notice that verse 15 speaks of God's love for *you*. Here Jesus describes the difference between a friend and a servant, and His choice for you. Verse 17 tells of God's love for *others* expressed through you. Sandwiched between them is God's mission for you.

2. Why is the love God has for you and for others significant in your life-to-life relationships?

3. Read Acts 26:16-18 and answer the following questions based on what you discover there.

   a. What action words convey the urgency of the Lord's mission for Saul (see verse16)? Do you consider God's call on your life to be urgent?

   b. Describe Saul's role to be in the mission the Lord was calling him to? What is your role in the mission to which He calls you?

   c. What did the Lord say Saul could expect the outcomes of his ministry to be (see verse 18)?

d. Do these verses motivate you to make life-to-life ministry a priority? How?

4. Read John 17:20-21. In the passage, how does Jesus see the world being reached?

Just think—you were in Jesus' prayers before you were even born.

5. Read 1 Thessalonians 3:1-6 and notice the "spiritual generations" represented in these verses.

   a. In Timothy's life-to-life relationship with the Thessalonians, what did he do to prepare them during a difficult time in their Christian walk?

b. What are some circumstances you have experienced that discouraged you?

c. Can you think of someone who "strengthened and encouraged" you during those times? What did they do?

6. After reading 2 Timothy 3:10-17 and the seven descriptions of a disciple listed here, record to the right of each point how you see these qualities demonstrated in Paul and Timothy's life-to-life relationship.

I *ntentional:*   *Purposeful*_____

M *odel:*   *By example*_____

I *ntegrity:*   *Biblically consistent lifestyle* _____

T *eachable:*   *Willingness to learn* _____

A *vailable:*   *Making time for discipling* _____

T *ransparent:*   *Sharing our lives* _____

E *quipping:*   *Developing character, skill, and competence*_____

7. What other relational qualities could be part of life-to-life ministry?

8. Imagine you are discipling a woman who shows signs of being unteachable
   or unavailable. Even with your godly counsel for her, she resists change. She
   also keeps canceling appointments with you, making excuses. How would you
   address these obstacles to her growth?

WRITINGS ALONG THE WAY

Finding the Right Person to Disciple

by Becky Brodin[2]

"You know what, Kathy? I think you're ready to disciple someone."

"Really?" she responded, blinking in surprise. "Do you think I could do it?"

I'd been discipling Kathy for more than a year. She had a sensitive heart, a deep desire to know the Lord, and an eagerness to learn. I knew that if she could help a younger believer grow, her understanding of discipleship would soar.

Then she asked, "Who should I disciple?" She was unfamiliar with one-to-one discipleship.

Because many people we might want to disciple are similar to Kathy, we have to take the initiative to begin a discipling relationship. Finding someone to disciple requires three things:

- involvement with people,
- knowing what to look for,
- and a willingness to take initiative.

Pools of People

To find someone to disciple, you need to be involved with people.

In our culture, this usually happens in some kind of small group, such as a Bible study or a Sunday school class.

When Jesus selected His disciples, He preached, healed, ministered, and soon had a group of people following Him. Then, after a night of prayer, He called his disciples to Him and chose twelve of them, whom He also designated apostles (Luke 6:13). Jesus was involved with people before He connected with them individually. They knew Him, and He knew them.

The Right Stuff

What an interesting mix of men Jesus chose as His disciples! Laborers, political zealots, educated professionals. He looked past their personalities and professions for deeper qualities.

Years ago, a wise mentor told me to be patient with this step of the process. He suggested looking for someone who is hungry to grow and instructed me to wait and watch for four to six months before I approached someone. When I asked him how I could tell, he assured me I would know. He was right. Those who wanted to grow:

- were committed to fellowship,
- studied on their own,
- and took the initiative to develop relationships.

Though this list may seem subjective, it's a good place to start. It will help you identify those who are interested in spiritual growth and those who will follow through.

Kathy had been involved in her groups for several months. When I asked her who seemed spiritually hungry, she named two people from her Bible study. She wanted to connect with both of them immediately. But I convinced her to pray about it, following Jesus' example.

After she'd done so, she was ready to take the next step.

Taking the Plunge

A discipling relationship is unique. It's personal. And it can be demanding, intense, time consuming, and life changing. Launching such a relationship requires initiative and honesty.

Luke 5:27-28 describes how Jesus recruited Matthew [also known as Levi]: *"After this, Jesus went out and saw a tax collector by the name of Levi sitting at his tax booth. 'Follow me,' Jesus said to him, and Levi got up, left everything and followed him."* The word *follower* in the Greek describes someone who seeks to be like his teacher, a companion who is "going in the same way." When Jesus called His disciples to follow Him, they knew what it meant. Whenever people chose to follow a particular teacher, they often left their jobs and current way of life to do so.

When Kathy and I talked about how to begin her relationship with someone she wanted to disciple, I suggested that she clearly describe the discipleship process. What she was asking of these women would require a commitment of time and purpose. I urged Kathy to be honest about it all. Kathy and I had begun our relationship the same way.

On the Lookout

Kathy met with both people for more than two years. Then each of them began discipling others. But Kathy didn't stop there. She continues to watch for people who are hungry to grow, takes the initiative to relate to them, and invites them into a unique adventure of one-to-one discipleship.

 TIPS FOR THE ROAD

One of the qualities of life-to-life relationships from the acronym IMITATE is transparency, which means that we openly share our lives, both our weaknesses and our strengths, with another person. We can set the tone for our relationships, whether in a group or one-to-one, by the level of our own transparency. Vulnerability is different than transparency. Vulnerability means that not only are we transparent but we allow others to speak into our lives. When we are vulnerable, we live out another quality: being teachable (see IMITATE list).

Early in your discipling relationship with another person, share some of your own struggles with sin. For example, you may be able to share about a time you were angry with a family member and needed to ask for that person's forgiveness. Being vulnerable might open the door for the person you are discipling to share some of her struggles. As you keep each other's confidence and pray for one another, transparency and vulnerability will grow.

It will probably be a relief to both of you when you make it clear that you are not perfect. Transparency breaks down barriers of perfectionism as both you and your disciple face the truth that you have not reached perfection and never will. As Paul said in Philippians 3:12, *"Not that I have already obtained all this, or have already been made perfect, but I press on to take hold of that for which Christ Jesus took hold of me."*

Don't hide behind a mask of perfection. Honest sharing will free both you and your disciple to share and to resist the temptation to compare. Your life will be blessed as you experience the joy of a life-to-life relationship in which both you and your disciple can grow in your relationships with the Lord.

Ask God to show you how you can be more transparent and vulnerable in your relationships, especially with the women He is calling you to disciple.

LEARNING THE ROUTE BY HEART

Connecting with God's power and promises is your moment-by-moment privilege as His daughter. As you memorize Philippians 1:3-4 for the next session, remember also to pray God's promises for any women you disciple.

Topic: God's Promises and Power

I thank my God every time I remember you. In all my prayers for all of you, I always pray with joy.

(PHILIPPIANS 1:3-4)

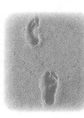

Next Steps on the Journey

Complete these items before the next meeting:
- Read and complete "Session 4: The Priority of Prayer."
- Read Acts 8-10 and come prepared to share a recent devotional highlight from your journal.
- Memorize Philippians 1:3-4 and review the verses from previous sessions.
- Be prepared to discuss thoughts on becoming more vulnerable in discipling relationships.
- In your journal, write down any answers you have seen to your prayers for the women you hope to disciple.

THE PRIORITY OF PRAYER

"HOW CAN I EXPERIENCE GOD'S POWER AND PROMISES?"

I thank my God every time I remember you.
In all my prayers for all of you, I always pray with joy.
(PHILIPPIANS 1:3-4)

So far in *Friends on the Journey* you have studied the value of developing a discipling vision, the Great Commission, and ministering life-to-life. In this session, you will discover that prayer is foundational to the entire discipling process; God's power holds it all together.

One of our privileges as God's daughters is to develop a connection with God's power and promises day by day, hour by hour, and minute by minute—in the good times as well as in the difficult times. Through prayer we have access to the resources God is longing to give us, if only we would ask.

The Lord (earnestly) waits—expecting, looking and longing—to be gracious to you; and therefore He lifts Himself up, that He may have mercy on you and show lovingkindness to you. For the Lord is a God of justice. Blessed—happy, fortunate and to be envied—are all those who (earnestly) wait for Him, who expect and look and long for Him (for His victory, His favor, His love, His peace, His joy, and His matchless, unbroken companionship).
(Isaiah 30:18, AMP)

We invite you to seek intimacy with God through prayer and dependence on His promises.

MY DAILY JOURNEY

In your journal, write out thoughts from your devotional times: what you are learning about God or yourself, how these truths can help you grow deeper in relationship with Him, and how you can demonstrate His love to others.

OUR JOURNEY TOGETHER

In your group:

- Share a recent highlight from your personal devotional times.
- Review together your memory verse, Philippians 1:3-4.
- Share from your journal how the Lord answered a recent prayer.
- Discuss together what you have learned about vulnerability in relationships.

Reflections from the Heart of a Discipler

"Influencing Others Through Prayer," by Ruth Fobes

When I was a young Christian, my mentor invited me to attend a conference with her. Prayer was the theme for the weekend, an area in which I longed to grow because I wanted to go deeper in my relationship with Jesus. What made this conference even more special to me was that I was going to meet the conference speaker, the woman who had discipled my mentor. I had heard so much about Joyce and the influence she'd had on so many women's lives. I could hardly wait.

When Joyce stood to speak, I was ready with pen and paper, eager to learn all

I could about this vital subject, but to my surprise she took an entirely different approach than I'd anticipated. Rather than teach us about prayer, she sent us out to do it. She said, "We talk a lot about prayer, but today I want you to *experience* prayer. Experience will be your best teacher. While we're at these beautiful conference grounds, I invite you to find a spot where you can settle in for an hour and just talk to God. If you don't know what to say, simply say, 'Lord, teach me to pray.'"

Eagerly, I found a spot under a big shade tree. *Where do I begin?* I thought. *I don't know how to pray effectively, or maybe I don't know how to pray at all.*

I began saying out loud, "Lord, teach me to pray." I prayed this over and over throughout the rest of that hour. I can't explain how He did it, but that day, God burned within my heart a passion to pray and to pursue prayer as a lifeline between God and me. By challenging me to actually pray instead of just teaching me about it, Joyce profoundly influenced my life.

In the days ahead, I continued to ask God to develop my ability to talk with and listen to Him. He faithfully answered, providing me with several key ideas and tools that have helped me grow in my convictions about prayer. He started by leading me to journal my prayers, a habit I continue to this day. As I write out my prayers along with what I sense Him saying to me, I experience God's blessing and encouragement. Journaling reveals in black and white how God answers my prayers. My journals also record history for future generations — a testimony to the power, grace, and love of God.

Praying God's characteristics back to Him is another practice God has given me to enhance my praying. As I read God's Word, I look for His attributes. Then I praise Him for that attribute. When I lift my sights and focus on the Lord, it causes my own concerns to be minimized.

One of the most exciting things God taught me about prayer is to rely on His promises and claim them for myself and for others. I used to just memorize verses, but a friend challenged me to pray them into my life and into the lives of others as well.

The first time I tried this, I took a walk with God and asked Him to make the verse I had memorized true of my life. I couldn't get that verse out of my mind all day and throughout the evening hours. I was thrilled to experience God fulfilling

His promise. The next day I prayed the same Scripture for a friend. Later that same day she told me, "The Lord keeps bringing this Scripture verse to mind. It has encouraged me all day." *Wow! It's working!* I thought. *It's changing my life, and it's impacting my friend's life. God is allowing me to be an influence for His sake, just like Joyce, and just like my mentor has been to me.* And that experience motivated me to pray Scripture for myself and for the women I'm discipling.

Learning to pray has been critical to my effectiveness in discipling. As I pray for the people I disciple, my prayers activate the power of God and allow me to partner with His Spirit to bring them growth. I couldn't be a discipler apart from prayer. I'm so glad I learned many years ago that the best way to learn to pray is by doing it.

———————————————

THE TRAVEL GUIDE

In the story you just read, you see that Ruth learned several key points about prayer. The most valuable lesson she learned was how important it is for her to stay connected to her power source, Jesus.

Imagine what journaling prayer could look like in your life. Journal your prayers for the next seven days, and then share with the group any blessings or encouragement that come from doing so.

1. Read Psalm 145, looking for God's attributes. Which attribute means the most to you? Talk to God about it in a short prayer written here. See David's prayer in 1 Chronicles 29:10-13 for an example of praying God's attributes.

2. Read the following verses with yourself and the people you are discipling in mind. Fill in the chart with the things you thank God for, the things you are asking Him for, and what you hope He will accomplish. Consider journaling your prayers and watch God's power at work as you pray exactly what is on His heart.

Scriptures	Thankful For	Prayed For	Desired Results
Ephesians 1:15-19			
1 Thessalonians 1:2-3			
2 Thessalonians 1:3-4			
2 Thessalonians 1:11-12			

God shapes the world by prayers. Prayers are deathless.
The lips that uttered them may be closed in death,
the heart that felt them may have ceased to beat,
but prayers live before God, and God's heart is set on them,
and prayers outlive the lives of those who uttered them;
outlive a generation, outlive an age, outlive a world.
—E. M. Bounds, *The Necessity of Prayer*

3. Jesus modeled prayer. Sometimes He spent whole nights in prayer. John 17:6-26 is a recorded prayer of Jesus for His disciples and for us. Through prayer you, too, can reach into the future, laying a foundation of blessing for those new disciples you are befriending and to generations beyond them. Study this prayer as you did the prayers in the previous question and fill in the chart with the things you are praying for yourself and others.

SCRIPTURES	THANKFUL FOR	PRAYED FOR	DESIRED RESULTS
John 17:6-26			

A promise is an oral or written agreement to do or not do something. God's promises, which are found throughout Scripture, are foundational to living and ministering in God's kingdom. God consistently uses promises for a variety of reasons, such as to guide, reveal His will, and encourage. You can bring His power into your discipling relationships when you live by faith according the promises of God.

God gives us His promises in order to awaken hope and expectation in us that will cause us to reach out through prayer and receive His gifts. As we pray His Word, we are simply activating what He has already made available: His power and provision.

4. Can you recall a time when you took God at His Word and believed one of His promises? What was the promise and what happened?

5. Read Romans 4:20-21, Hebrews 6:17-18, and 2 Peter 1:3-4. What do you think God wants us to gain from His promises?

6. What promises stand out to you from Scripture?

Living by God's promises means identifying what He has promised to us and then living in light of that promise. Doing this involves faith and obedience. The following are five questions that can help us understand and live by His promises. Answering these questions well will put you in a position to receive the good things God intends for you and for those you disciple.

- **Who made the promise?** Behind God's promises are His character and resources. The principle of living by the promises of God is powerful because God's character guarantees that the thing promised will in fact happen. The very foundation of our Christian faith rests on what God has said — that He completes His commitments. God's ability and resources are limitless, making His promises sure. For instance, Numbers 23:19 says that God does not lie or change His mind, Proverbs 30:5 says that every word of God is flawless, and Matthew 24:35 says that His words will never pass away.
- **What is the promise?** Understanding what God has actually said and meant in His promises is critical to living by them. Usually the context of the promise helps us know His meaning.
- **Who is the promise for?** Living by God's promises requires that we identify to whom the promise was given. Some promises were given to specific individuals.

Some are for a specific time and others for any time. However, much of what God promises is still intended for us today. If we fail to recognize these promises, we miss experiencing God's blessing and design. His promises ignite our faith and shape our lives as they claim us.

- **What are the conditions?** The main condition regarding the promises of God is faith. Sometimes there are other conditions as well. Conditions are to promises as planting and cultivating are to seeds. They don't cause the growth but they do make it possible. Every promise requires faith that ultimately is based on the character of God. As Hebrews 11:6 says, "Without faith it is impossible to please God, because anyone who comes to him must believe that he exists and that he rewards those who earnestly seek him."

- **What endurance is required?** God rarely gives and fulfills His promises at the same time. Waiting is often part of God's pattern for living by promises: "You need to persevere so that when you have done the will of God, you will receive what he has promised" (Hebrews 10:36).

7. Look at the following passages and note what the promise was and who the recipients are.

   a. Acts 2:38-39

   b. Romans 4:16-17

c. Ephesians 3:6

8. From the following passages, note the promise and the condition.

a. Proverbs 3:5-6

b. Joshua 1:8

c. John 16:24

Promises from God, at least for me, do not come from
casual flipping through the Bible, but rather they are born out
of conflict and struggle. They are born out of much prayer
and time in the Word. Remember that you don't obey
a promise; you believe it. God makes it happen,
you don't. Because of His promises we obey His commands.
We believe a promise. We obey a command.
—Lorne Sanny, former president of The Navigators

9. Ministry often begins with a word or promise from God. Why should you pray God's promises for your ministry of discipling others?

10. What promises are you praying by faith for your life and ministry?

WRITINGS ALONG THE WAY

Living by God's Promises

by Skip Gray[1]

Claiming God's promises is the heart of our prayer life. We simply take back to God His promises of what He said He would do. As we appropriate God's promises by faith, we enrich our communication with Christ, our trust and adoration of Him, and our obedience to Him. This is a lifetime process. The better we get to know Him—seeing Him make and keep promises—the greater confidence we'll have in His trustworthiness as the years go by.

The Bible contains two kinds of promises: *general* promises, which apply to all Christians at all times under all circumstances; and *specific* promises, which apply only in certain situations.

Examples of general promises are:

- 1 John 5:11-12: "God has given us eternal life, and this life is in his Son."
- 1 John 1:9: "If we confess our sins, he is faithful and just and will forgive us our sins and purify us from all unrighteousness."

Specific Promises: God frequently gives guidance and direction to individual Christians in particular areas of life in a way that doesn't apply to the entire body of Christ or to all the Christians in a given community. Here are several guidelines to remember in specific promises that can keep us from drifting off into error, imbalance, or some other harmful and subjective application.

First, many promises have the condition of our obedience to God.

Second, God will never lead you through one verse of Scripture to do something He clearly prohibits somewhere else in the Scriptures. Keep in mind the total witness of the Scriptures whenever you use a particular promise as the basis for making a decision.

Third, don't decide when and how a promise must be fulfilled. God wants us to know that He's loving, kind, wise, and gracious. He wants us to believe He's like this whether or not He answers our prayers the way we had in mind.

Fourth, present your need to God in prayer, and let God pick out the promise. At some point in time the Holy Spirit will impress you as you're moving through God's Word. He'll say, "This is for you."

Finally, remember that God makes and keeps promises for His glory—that all the peoples of the earth may know that the Lord is God (1 Kings 8:60).

 TIPS FOR THE ROAD

What are you praying for the women you are discipling? From the following Scriptures (or other Scriptures God has given you), select a few verses to pray into the lives of the women you are influencing.

A Transformed Life

Romans 12:2: That she would be transformed by the renewing of her mind.

Philippians 1:9-11: That her love may abound in knowledge and depth of insight; that she would be able to discern.

2 Peter 1:3-4: That God's power would help her escape the corruption in the world caused by evil desires.

Passion and Trust for God

Psalm 34:4-5: That she would seek the Lord, hear His answers and be freed from fear; that she would look to Him and be radiant.

Philippians 4:6-7: That she would no longer be anxious but would present her requests to God and receive His peace.

Hope, Joy, Love, Peace, and Strength

Romans 5:3-5: That she would allow suffering to produce in her godly perseverance, character, and hope that does not disappoint.

Psalm 29:11: That the Lord would give her strength and bless her with peace.

Isaiah 61:3: The Lord would give her a crown of beauty along with gladness and praise and that she will be called an oak of righteousness

Life Direction

Psalm 119:133-135: That God would direct her footsteps according to His Word and let no sin rule over her.

Proverbs 3:5-6: That she would trust in the Lord and not in her own understanding; that He will direct her paths.

Wisdom and Knowledge of Christ Jesus

Ephesians 1:17-19: That God will give her wisdom to know Him better, along with understanding, hope, and His great power.

Obedience to God

2 Corinthians 10:5: That God would help her to demolish argument that prevents her from knowing Him fully and teach her how to make every thought obedient to Christ.

Isaiah 57:15: That God would help her develop a contrite and lowly spirit that invites His presence.

Ministering to Others

John 15:5: That she would remain in Jesus, bear much fruit, and not try to do anything apart from Him.

1 Corinthians 15:58: That she would give herself fully to the Lord so that her labor is not in vain.

LEARNING THE ROUTE BY HEART

Spiritual disciplines are heart habits that are critical to spiritual growth and for finishing well. As you memorize your verse for the next session, pray that God will help you become more disciplined for the purpose of seeking a more intimate relationship with Him.

Topic: Spiritual Discipline

Train yourself to be godly. For physical training is of some value, but godliness has value for all things, holding promise for both the present life and the life to come.

(1 TIMOTHY 4:7-8)

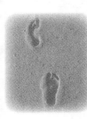

Next Steps on the Journey

Complete these items before the next meeting:

- Read and complete "Session 5: Essentials for the Journey."
- Memorize 1 Timothy 4:7-8 and review the verses from previous sessions.
- Read Acts 11-13 and come prepared to share a recent devotional highlight from your journal.
- Ask the Lord to give you Scriptures you can pray for your life as well as pray into the lives of the women with whom you are building discipling friendships.

ESSENTIALS FOR THE JOURNEY

"WHAT ARE GOOD HABITS FOR A SPIRITUALLY HEALTHY HEART?"

*Train yourself to be godly. For physical training is of some value,
but godliness has value for all things, holding promise for both
the present life and the life to come.*

(1 TIMOTHY 4:7-8)

In the last session, we learned that prayer is a privilege that gives us access to God's power and promises for the disciplemaking process. In this session, we will see that spiritual discipline is critical to finishing well on our journey of discipleship.

We invite you to enjoy the blessings that come from being faithful in your spiritual disciplines. These good habits will provide an environment where God can create a spiritually healthy heart.

MY DAILY JOURNEY

In your journal, write out thoughts from your devotional times: what you are learning about God or yourself, how these truths can help you grow deeper in relationship with Him, and how you can demonstrate His love to others.

OUR JOURNEY TOGETHER

In your group:

- Share a recent highlight from your personal devotional times.
- Review together your memory verse, 1 Timothy 4:7-8.
- Share with your group the Scriptures you are praying for the women you are discipling.

Reflections from the Heart of a Discipler

"Burning Bright or Burning Out?" by Gigi Busa

I was in major burnout. After discipling women for eight years, I was asked to teach and equip other churches to intentionally disciple their congregations. I should have been excited about this new opportunity to minister, but I had never been trained for this type of teaching and was unsure of even where to start. This new assignment meant that in addition to serving on staff at my own church and being a full-time homemaker, mom, and chauffeur to my three children with their many activities, I would now be developing a seminar and traveling many miles to teach twice a month.

The idea was overwhelming. My physical and emotional capacity was already stretched thin, and I was finding little joy in serving or even in my time with Jesus. What had happened to my passion for Him?

I knew I needed spiritual refreshing, so I signed up for the first retreat I could find. God fully knew my needs, so He arranged for the speaker, author and women's discipler Cynthia Heald, to spend five life-changing minutes with me. She asked specific and probing questions: "How much time do you spend in the Word?" "Where are you reading?" "What ministries are you involved in at home and church?"

Her counsel surprised me. The problem wasn't my ministry load or lack of training, she said. "Don't stop serving. God is using you. The problem is you are giving out much more than you are taking in. Increase your time with the Lord. I suggest that you get alone with Him for an entire day once a month."

I took her advice to heart and carved out time the very next week. In that time alone with God, I evaluated my life, examined my schedule, and prayed for direction. I reflected on my personal purpose statement and life goals.

Although it's important to me that my activities reflect God's purpose for my life, without any effort my life resembled a junk drawer, cluttered and unorganized. In order for the Lord to use me more effectively, I needed to de-clutter my life. Not that anything I was doing was bad, but if I wanted my life to be full of the excellent, I had to eliminate a great number of the merely good things. I realized that my life did not have to be out of control; I needed to learn to make choices that would bring my schedule under control. I asked the Lord, "What can I do? What can I delegate and train others to do? What must stop, even if there is no one to take it over?"

These monthly retreats are now a consistent part of my life. My goal is to live within God's plan for my life (see 2 Corinthians 10:13, NLT). These times with God are crucial to helping me stay true to that goal. Now when I am asked to serve in a way that will take a good part of my time, I have learned to say, "Let me pray about it for a few weeks." Then I take that request before God on my next monthly getaway and allow Him to direct the answer.

I've learned that the closer I get to God, the more opportunities for ministry will be open to me. I need to discern God's plan for my life before accepting the invitations that will come. He doesn't expect me to be the answer to every ministry need; perhaps He has another woman in mind that He will use more effectively and she will grow as a result of the challenge. I am learning not to be moved by my emotions or the needs of a ministry but to stop, wait, and listen for His voice, for He knows the ministry need and my future far better than I.

Another benefit of these monthly retreats is that during the long hours of solitude, God uncovers and peels away the calluses on my heart caused by busyness, distractions, sin, bad attitudes, or fears. I ask Him to show me anything that has interfered with my intimacy with Him. I ask Him, "Where do I see You at work in my life, in my family, in my church, in the women I disciple? Am I in step with You?" Sometimes it takes hours for my mind and heart to become quiet enough to hear His whispers, but He always works faithfully through His Word and the Holy Spirit to expose areas that need His touch and to transform me, starting from within my heart to my thoughts, my words, and my actions.

Is a day of solitude a luxury? Gail MacDonald, in her book *A Step Farther and Higher*,[1] helped me gain perspective on this. She watched as a farmer and his wife, swinging their scythes in rhythm, cut mountain grass in the Alps. Routinely they would stop, take a rock out of their pockets, and sharpen their blades. Couldn't they take fewer breaks to sharpen and get more accomplished? Gail observed that this time of sharpening was not a break in their work; it was actually part of their work. Similarly, if you and I want to grow closer to Christ, we, too, must take regular breaks to let God sharpen us.

Disciplines, such as my days of solitude, are indispensable in giving my soul room to breathe and grow as I sink my roots deeper in Christ. What I learn from the Lord in these times keeps me on the right path when (not if) life's most difficult experiences come. Over the years, I have learned that as I take intentional time to focus on Him and listen for His whispers, I practice a holy habit that invites Him to direct my paths rather than have my ways dictated by others' demands or my own human desires. Life is too short to burn out or to miss the very best God has planned for me!

THE TRAVEL GUIDE

Spiritual disciplines are practices that encourage spiritual growth. In Gigi's story, we observe the value of solitude, silence, and reflection.

Throughout this journey of discipleship, you have studied the disciplines of prayer, reading, studying, memorizing, meditating, and applying Scriptures to your life, as well as learning to share the gospel and developing skills to serve others. You are well on your way to developing a spiritually healthy heart. Being grounded in these spiritual habits helps you make the most of your opportunities to encourage and disciple others as you continue on your own journey.

As Gigi learned, development of new spiritual disciplines was crucial to restoring her joy in Christ and her passion for ministry. Disciplines, such as goal setting, simplicity, stewardship, and worship gave her energy to minister from the overflow of her time with Christ.

Discipline requires cultivation. In biblical terms, discipline is training or exercising.

1. What do the following passages teach us about spiritual training or exercise?
   a. 1 Corinthians 9:24-27

   b. 1 Timothy 4:6-12

   c. Hebrews 12:1-3,11

Discipline brings freedom. One important benefit to developing spiritual discipline is that it enables us to respond to unpredicted circumstances in our lives with godly actions. How we act during a moment of stress or crisis can affect the short-term or long-term consequences we experience, for better or for worse.

2. In Daniel 6:3-10, what aspects of spiritual discipline does Daniel demonstrate? What benefits do those godly habits allow him to enjoy?

3. In Mark 14:37-38, Jesus admonishes Peter for sleeping when He had asked him to be alert and pray. He reminds Peter, "The spirit is willing, but the body is weak." Later, Peter proves Jesus right when he denies Him three times. What lesson do you think Jesus wanted Peter to learn? Have you ever experienced a time when your spirit was willing but your flesh was weak? Explain how spiritual disciplines could help at a time like this.

Good habits produce a spiritually healthy heart, but discipline in itself could become legalism, which is an outward adherence to a set of rules without an inward change of heart. Jesus criticized the Pharisees many times for this. In Matthew 23:23, Jesus calls them hypocrites. Spiritual habits in themselves do not make us godly, but they do place us in an environment where God can address issues of our heart.

4. Read the following passages and then finish this statement for each: Habits can enslave us when . . .

a. Isaiah 29:13

b. Matthew 7:1-5

c. Matthew 12:9-14

5. How can you keep discipline from becoming an enslaving habit?

6. In what ways have you seen discipline lead to more freedom in your life?

There is a delicate balance between God's grace and self-discipline. We never earn God's love by the things we do. His love is *always* unconditional. The disciplines do not cause God to love you more. Also, the disciplines themselves do not change you; rather, they are practices that can put you in God's presence and Word so that He can transform you. Spiritual growth is not about having seven quiet times a week and memorizing verses; it comes when we use these means to increasingly live our lives as Jesus would.

2 Peter 1:3-8 demonstrates this balance between grace and discipline:

His divine power has given us everything we need for life and godliness . . . so that through them you may participate in the divine nature and escape the corruption in the world . . . For this very reason [you] make every effort to add to your faith, goodness, and to goodness knowledge, and to knowledge self-control . . . for if you possess these qualities in increasing measure, they will keep you from being ineffective and unproductive in your knowledge of our Lord Jesus Christ.

In this section, you will be introduced to the spiritual discipline of goal setting. Goal setting helps you to steward your life and make the most of it.

Goal Setting

Without vision and goals, our lives often become routine. Like a gerbil in a wheel, we move frantically but don't get anywhere. The Bible commands us to live differently. In Ephesians 5:15-17, Paul says, *"Be very careful, then, how you live, not as unwise but as wise, making the most of every opportunity, because the days are evil. . . . Understand what the Lord's will is."* In 1 Corinthians 9:26, he tells us, "Do not run . . . aimlessly." And in Romans 14:12, he reminds us that "each of us will give an account of himself to God."

Goals give us a framework to practice the stewardship of our time and give direction and motivation to fulfill the plans He has for our lives. Goals should be challenging, measurable, and specific.

How do we set goals? First of all, pray! Carve out a day to hear clearly from Him.

The more you pray and work on your goals, the more in tune you will become to God and His leading.

The following exercise will guide your prayers and thoughts. Jot down ideas as they come to mind.

Picture yourself ten or even twenty years from now:

- What qualities or characteristics would you want people to use to describe you?
- Describe your relationship with the Lord.
- What are your priorities and values?

At your current age:

- What is your passion? What excites you and gives you joy to talk about or do?
- Is there a dream God has placed on your heart? If time and money were not a restraint, what would you do?
- What bothers you about yourself or your circumstances that you can change?

Pray over these thoughts and organize them into categories: Spiritual, Family, Ministry, Personal, and Career. Think of at least one goal for each category. Here are some examples:

- **Spiritual:** To be a lifelong learner, always growing in my love, knowledge, and service to Jesus
- **Ministry:** To always be discipling and to pass my discipling vision on to others
- **Personal:** To stay in shape mentally and physically so I can complete my God-given tasks

In the following chart, list your goals. Pray about the steps you can take in the next three months to bring you closer to each goal. Make a copy of the list to post in a place where you will be reminded daily to pray for God's direction and empowerment.

CATEGORY	GOALS	THE STEPS I WILL TAKE IN THE NEXT THREE MONTHS TO REACH THESE GOALS
Spiritual		
Family		
Ministry		
Personal		
Career		

Goal setting is just one of the many spiritual disciplines you can use to cultivate your relationship with Jesus. Holy habits should focus on your love for Him and not be a to-do list. Your relationship with Jesus needs what any other relationship needs in order to grow: quality and quantity time spent together. An intimate relationship does not just happen; it is intentionally built.

WRITINGS ALONG THE WAY

Is Fasting Relevant for Today's Christian?

by Gigi Busa

In our affluent and self-indulgent culture, self-denial in any form is a radical thought. But fasting has value for today's Christians. To deny oneself of food for the purpose of being more attentive to God is an act of humility and dependence on Him.

Fasting helps us to focus on God intentionally in order to seek Him in a specific way. It is the voluntary abstinence of food for the purpose of godliness. The words in both the Greek, *nesteia*, and the Hebrew, *tsom*, refer to self-denial. Different types of fasting were commanded in the Bible, and it was also a discipline Jesus taught and practiced. There were national fasts, such as the one described in 2 Chronicles 20:3; congregational fasts, as mentioned in Acts 13:2; and private fasts, such as in Jesus' forty days in the desert (see Matthew 4). Jesus assumes that we, too, will fast (see Matthew 6:16-18).

There are several types of fasts:

- In a "normal fast," a person abstains from all food but not water.
- A "partial fast" involves the abstention from only certain foods, for example meat or dessert.
- An "absolute fast" means a person is abstaining from all food and beverage.

These are several purposes for fasting:

- To strengthen urgent prayer
- To seek God's guidance
- To seek deliverance from sin or evil

- To express repentance for sin
- To express devotion to God

A simple way to begin to practice this discipline is to fast from sundown one day to the sundown of the next day. Use the time you would normally spend in meal preparation and eating as time with God in prayer and reading Scriptures that refer to the purpose of your fast. (Consult your physician first if you have any special medical concerns.) Answering the following questions will help you make the most of your fast.

- When will I fast?
- What type of fast will I use?
- What is the purpose of the fast?
- What did I experience during this time?

 TIPS FOR THE ROAD

Use the following questionnaire at least once a year to help you evaluate your spiritual growth and where God may be leading you next on your walk with Him.

1. When you first met Christ, what were the indicators of your love for Him? How does your passion for Him compare today?

2. What are the major barriers to your growth in Christ?

     Unconfessed sin _____ Lack of discipline _____ Busyness _____
     Worry _____ Pursuit of my own agenda _____ Self-sufficiency _____
     Something else _____

3. On a scale of 1 to 10, one being the lowest, how would you rate yourself spiritually compared with last year?

     ____ I am more aware of and sensitive to God.
     ____ I place more importance on the spiritual disciplines,
            such as reading the Word.
     ____ I am more controlled by the Word and God's Spirit.
     ____ I am more aware of my sin.
     ____ I am more aware of others' needs.
     ____ I share Christ more frequently.

4. What is one area God is drawing your attention to? What will you do in the next month to address this? What can you do to keep this area a priority in your life?

The admission to the inner circle of intimacy is the outcome of deep desire.
Only those who count it a prize worth sacrificing anything else
for are likely to attain it. We are now, and will be in the future,
only as close to God as we really choose to be.
— J. Oswald Chambers, *Enjoying Intimacy with God*

LEARNING THE ROUTE BY HEART

Healing is vital for continued transformation on your journey and for the women you disciple. As you memorize your verse for the next session, reflect on how Jesus restored and brought healing to so many people. Jesus also offers healing and freedom for you and for the women you disciple.

Topic: Healing and Transformation

The Spirit of the Sovereign LORD is on me, because the LORD has anointed me to preach good news to the poor. He has sent me to bind up the brokenhearted, to proclaim freedom for the captives and release from darkness for the prisoners.

(ISAIAH 61:1)

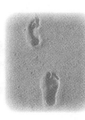

Next Steps on the Journey

Complete these items before the next meeting:

- Read and complete "Session 6: Lightening the Load."
- Memorize Isaiah 61:1 and review the verses from previous sessions.
- Read Acts 14-16 and come prepared to share a recent devotional highlight from your journal.
- Come prepared to share the goals God has led you to set.
- Share what the group can pray with you about (your joys and concerns) as you disciple others.

Session 6

LIGHTENING THE LOAD

"How can I help when a woman I disciple is emotionally wounded?"

*The Spirit of the Sovereign L*ORD *is on me,*
*because the L*ORD *has anointed me to preach good news*
to the poor. He has sent me to bind up the brokenhearted,
to proclaim freedom for the captives and release from darkness
for the prisoners.
(ISAIAH 61:1)

In session 5, we developed a sense of what it means to nurture habits of the heart and outline a life and ministry plan for ourselves. We see that these habits are essential to our own transformation. As we minister to women, however, we quickly discover that we cannot disciple women and ignore their areas of woundedness. In order to truly help women in the disciplemaking process and avoid burnout ourselves, we need clarity about our role in contrast to Jesus' role in the process of healing and transformation.

We invite you to look closely at Jesus' healing ministry and what it means for us as we come alongside women who are hurting.

MY DAILY JOURNEY

In your journal, write out thoughts from your devotional times: what you are learning about God or yourself, how these truths can help you grow deeper in relationship with Him, and how you can demonstrate His love to others.

OUR JOURNEY TOGETHER

In your group:

- Share a recent highlight from your personal devotional times.
- Review together your memory verse, Isaiah 61:1.
- Describe how the Lord has led you in setting goals.
- Give your group suggestions on how they can join you in praying for the women you are discipling. In your group interactions, be conscious of guarding the confidentiality of your women.

Reflections from the Heart of a Discipler

"The Painful Truth," by Diane Manchester

As I minister and disciple life-to-life with women, I consistently find that ministry is messy. The following vignettes express hurts that some women I discipled brought into our relationship. As I listened to these women, my heart ached for them; but initially I also felt a sense of helplessness. What could I say or do to ease their pain, to lighten their load?

———

Julie looked down in her lap as she shared. "I remember hearing my older sister cry out for help, but Mom had already left for work and I was too young to do anything." Julie was tormented with nightmares that reflected her feeling of powerlessness during her father's incestuous assaults upon her sister when they both were children. As Julie grew, she came to believe that she needed to protect herself from her dad's advances, so she became a fighter, able to defend herself whenever necessary. And she found ways to anesthetize the haunting sounds of her sister's cries.

———

Joy's eyes brimmed with tears, her hands twisting a well-used tissue. "I am anything but computer literate, but somehow I found these messages on our e-mail. I learned later that they came from a chat room that my husband frequently visited. I was stunned that some woman was suggesting he leave me, referring to me in very crude terms! At first, I felt paralyzed. My husband had another life about which I had known nothing. Then my anger moved me to confront him, only to learn that Internet pornography had led him to this chat room. He'd been hooked on porn for years! How can I ever forgive all that he has done to me and to our family, much less be intimate with him again? I can hardly compare to the women he's been looking at!"

———

"I know I need to let her work this out, between her and God, and that she is an adult, but it's hard for me to just let go!" Christine shared quietly, though her passion was evident. "After all I taught her about the sanctity of life, and now this: an abortion, and we didn't even know. What could I have done differently? I can't get out of my mind that somehow we must have failed her as parents."

———

As I've walked beside these women and others in emotional pain, God has lessened my sense of helplessness by teaching me some things that have enabled me to better minister to them. Following are three encouraging truths I've learned.

- **God can use my own woundedness to help me connect with others.** As I've dealt with my own pain from being part of an alcoholic family, I've been able to be more transparent and open with the women I disciple. Because I can empathize with their pain, I am better able to meet them at their points of need.
- **I cannot heal people.** When I feel burdened or discouraged in the process of discipling hurting women, it usually means I have stepped into Jesus' domain. I cannot heal them, but Jesus can. I need to point my struggling friends to Him.
- **The truth can set them free.** I ask God to give me the specific "words of life" He has for the needs of the women with whom I'm meeting. As they meditate on these Scriptures, God uses them to refute the false beliefs that dominate their thoughts and bring healing.

THE TRAVEL GUIDE

Most of us carry emotional baggage that to one degree or other keeps us enslaved to our painful past; perhaps our stories are similar to the women's in the vignettes Diane shared. But the good news is, Jesus Christ came to set captives free. He was anointed to heal and to free us.

The women we disciple sometimes carry heavy burdens, and how we respond to them can either lighten their loads or weigh them down even further. God can bring healing through us as we share words of faith, trust, and life to replace the Enemy's deceptions of doubt, self-sufficiency, and death.

The specifics of healing and transformation may look a little different for each of us. But in general, healing means the restoration of health, making whole or well whether physically, emotionally, or spiritually. What can we do as disciplemakers to help women in their healing processes as they grow in their relationship with Christ? We may not be trained therapists, but we can offer biblical guidance. So for this part of our journey, we will narrow our focus to three questions:

- How can I meet a woman at her point of need?
- What is my role and what is Christ's role in a woman's healing process?
- How can I help her to recognize the false beliefs that trap her in her pain and to claim the truth that sets her free?

How can I meet a woman at her point of need?

We recommend that before you begin this session with women you are discipling, you personally go through the Healing Prayer Worksheet under Tips for the Road. As you heal in your own wounds, you will be more effective in your ministry to hurting women.

1. Read John 4:1-42. Meditate on the passage, particularly noting how Jesus met this woman at her point of need. Today we might label her as having relationship addiction or as a woman who loved too much. Such labels look only at the surface events and not at the underlying hurts, needs, and motives of the women we disciple. Complete the following table with the insights God gives

you for applying Jesus' example to your ministry with a hurting person. Keep in mind that this passage is a great pattern for evangelistic ministry as well.

VERSES	TOPIC	JESUS' EXAMPLE	MY APPLICATION
4-15	Starting the conversation		
16-17	Challenging her lifestyle		
18-26	Illuminating truth versus false beliefs		
27-42	Outcomes: spiritual multiplication		

What is my role and what is Christ's role in a woman's healing process?

2. Read Matthew 4:24; 15:30; Luke 5:17-26. These passages distinguish a "division of labor" between people with hurting friends and Jesus, who could heal their friends. What is your role and what is Jesus' role? How could you fulfill that role with a particular woman?

3. Revisit Luke 5:17-26 and compare it with Isaiah 53:4-5 (prophecy of Christ on the cross).

a. In these passages, what are some indications that healing through Jesus Christ is more than just physical healing?

Hints: For what were the men who carried the paralytic commended? To what did the Pharisees object? What did Christ accomplish on the Cross?

---

b. How was Jesus empowered to heal (see Luke 5:17; Acts 10:38)?

c. How will you be empowered in your ministry (see John 14:26; 16:13)?

4. Read Luke 7:20-22. When disciples of John the Baptist came to Jesus, they relayed John's question, "Are you the expected one, or do we look for someone else?" (NASB). What evidence did Jesus use to reveal His identity and answer John's questions?

> **Note:** Jesus could have answered John the Baptist's questions in any number of ways. He could have said, for example: "I was born of a virgin." That fact made Him unique. But He also was unique in His miraculous healings—and it was the evidence of people healed by Him that Jesus used to convince John the Baptist and his followers that He indeed was the Christ. Likewise, His role as Healer is unique from our role as guides to Him.

5. If someone observed your ministry, what would they "go and report" (Luke 7:22)? Would they observe that you are a "rescuer" or "fixer" of women you disciple, or would they say that you encourage women to go to Jesus for healing? Give a concrete example of your ministry approach or of the approach you intend to take when a healing need comes up in your discipling ministry.

As "fixers," we take on the responsibility for another woman's healing. "Fixers" and "rescuers" are greatly in danger of ministry burnout!

> It is one thing to intellectually know God's Word. It is another thing to seek, under the guidance of the Holy Spirit, those passages that are *relevant* to women's struggles and to offer these "words of living water" to them.

How can I help her to recognize her false beliefs and to claim the truth that sets her free?

TRUE BELIEFS	FALSE BELIEFS?[1]
Are based on the truth and reality of God's Word	Are based on fear, loss, or pain
Increase the value and growth of an individual	Demean and diminish the value and growth of an individual
Are proven true through life experiences that edify both self and others	Are proven false by destructive, defensive behaviors and painful relationships
Result in safe, healthy relationships	Result in separation and isolation from others
Create peace and confidence	Create anxiety and exhaustion
Result in accurate emotional responses	Result in inappropriate emotional responses

6. From 2 Timothy 2:15,22-26, what counsel do I receive as a discipler? What are the responsibilities of disciplers? Of people being discipled?

7. How would you have gently instructed (see verse 25) someone who opposed you as you guided them in God's Word?

WRITINGS ALONG THE WAY

Healing the Brokenhearted

by Arlyn Lawrence[2]

Prayer for emotional healing is an important component of our ministry in the body of Christ. When we participate in it, we follow the example of Jesus, who ministered frequently to people's personal brokenness. His desire was to free them from the bondage of sin and heal them physically, spiritually, and emotionally.

The Spirit of the Lord is on me, because he has anointed me to preach good news to the poor. He has sent me to proclaim freedom for the prisoners and recovery of sight for the blind, to release the oppressed, to proclaim the year of the Lord's favor.

Jesus' healings were more than just physical and spiritual. Think of the immoral woman at the well (see John 4), who we can assume, judging by the uncharacteristic hour at which she drew water, lived an isolated life. Yet after her encounter with Jesus, she excitedly brought the whole community "streaming from the village to see him" (verse 30, NLT).

My friend "Marie" experienced this ministry when friends at church gathered to pray for her. Even after becoming a Christian, Marie struggled with deep-seated fear caused by childhood abuse and the accidental death of her infant son. She was afraid of everything and spent excessive time planning escape routes and defense strategies from imaginary dangers. She also lived with the lie that all these behaviors and emotions were just a part of her personality.

As Marie's friends prayed for her, they received an impression from the Holy Spirit that fear was not a component of her personality; rather, it was the result of areas of emotional woundedness that God desired to heal. They prayed for her to know the truth and that the truth would set her free (Jn. 8:32). They revisited painful experiences that had led to her fears and helped her to receive God's love, peace, and presence. They prayed spiritual warfare prayers against the enemy's schemes to exploit her fear and make it a stronghold in her life.

Marie distinctly felt a burden lift, and after that experience she started to take fearful thoughts captive (2 Cor. 10:5) so they no longer controlled her. Her healing continues today: When fear assails her, Marie is able to recognize it and resist it through prayer rather than allow it to dominate her.

THE HEALING PROCESS

There are few things that affect our perceptions of God, self, others, and the world around us as much as our emotions do. Marie was unable to trust or relate to God as the loving, protective Father that He is. Through others praying with and for her, she was set free by the truth and power of Jesus. Prayer for emotional healing radically altered Marie's ability to relate to God and others and to live in peace with herself.

There are three important things to remember about prayer ministry for emotional healing.

- Emotional healing is a process. Often God does His healing work in us through a series of prayer conversations—both alone and with others facilitating. After that, it is a continual process of being transformed by the renewing of our minds (Ro. 12:2).
- Emotional healing is often part of a bigger work of God in one's life. Our emotions are inextricably intertwined with our bodies, minds, and spirits. It is rare that emotional healing can occur independently of other kinds of healing, such as spiritual and physical.
- Prayer for healing of any kind is something we as believers should do for one another (James 5:16). We are a body (1 Corinthians 12). Praying for one another for healing is an important part of Christian life.

COMPONENTS OF ONE-ANOTHER PRAYER

1. **Addressing the lies and work of the enemy.** The enemy builds strongholds of deception that become habitual thought patterns, personality characteristics, and negative behaviors (Ephesians 4:27; 1 Peter 5:8). We can use the authority given to us by Jesus (Luke 10:19; James 4:7) to rebuke and resist it directly.

2. **Hearing God's voice.** Listening prayer is important. The Holy Spirit knows our deepest thoughts as well as the thoughts of those we seek to help. He is uniquely able to identify lies that stand in the way of His healing.

3. **Receiving God's love.** The purpose of healing prayer is not the relief of symptoms but to release wounded people to experience the love and presence of the Father so they can enjoy Him and be a vessel of His love to others.

4. **Repenting of sin.** Biblical repentance means completely turning away from sinful patterns of behavior and embracing patterns of wholeness, obedience, and righteousness.

5. **Forgiving offenders.** Forgiving doesn't mean acting as if the wrong never happened. It means releasing our offenders from the debt they owe us because of the hurt we experienced at their hands. Doing so is one of the most crucial components of prayer for emotional healing.

6. **Affirming truth.** Jesus said that it is truth that sets us free (Jn. 8:32). Because many emotional wounds are related to lies we have believed about ourselves, it is important to declare what God thinks and says about us and to hear these truths affirmed and reaffirmed by others.

7. **Laying on hands.** When we lay hands on others as we pray for them, we become vessels through which God's Spirit can flow in a tangible way.

Whether on the giving or the receiving end, we are doing what Jesus did—just as He said we would (John 14:12). We are living out the desire of His heart that we be saved and delivered, healed and whole—not just in the next life, but starting today.

 TIPS FOR THE ROAD

This section offers a framework for listening to God and laying before Him your areas of repetitive emotional pain. In spending time in His presence, you have an opportunity to ask God to reveal the truth that will set you free from lies connected with painful experiences in your life. The following steps will guide you through the healing process:[3]

- Ask God to reveal to you a painful emotion that has high impact upon your thoughts and behavior.
- Listen to God as you ask, "Lord, when was the first time I experienced this emotion?" Allow yourself to feel pain connected with this memory.
- Ask God to show you any lies connected with this memory, false beliefs you came to believe. Consider both *projected* and *survival* lies. Projected lies are based on untruths that other people have told you about yourself (for example, "You're just like your drunken mother"). Survival lies are lies you have told yourself, especially as a child, in order to survive difficult or abusive situations (such as "I don't need anyone").
- Wait patiently in listening prayer as you ask God, "What is Your truth that will set me free from this lie?"
- Ask God to show you Jesus' presence and what He was doing or feeling at the time of this painful experience.
- Hearing God can be blocked by your not fully forgiving the one(s) who wounded you, your not fully forgiving yourself (for not accepting what Christ did on the cross for you), or any anger at God for allowing your experience. You can exercise forgiveness by praying, for example,

> Lord, I now choose to forgive _____ for
> _____ . I choose to release my hurt and anger and
> to release _____ . In the authority and name of the
> Lord Jesus Christ, I take back any ground I allowed
> Satan to gain in my life because of unforgiveness. In
> Jesus' name. Amen.

- Ask God, "Were there any unbiblical vows I made in the wounding event to protect myself from pain?" When we are hurt, we often make vows such as "I will never . . ." As you listen, if God reveals any vows you have made to protect yourself, pray specifically to renounce each vow in the name of Jesus Christ.

- In listening prayer, ask God to show you any emotional burdens you need to place at Jesus' feet. Release those burdens to Him in prayer. Truly surrender this time to the Lord, trusting that He will reveal what you need at the moment. Avoid attempting to control this time with your own efforts. Journal all God reveals to you. May you gain true freedom as you continue to practice listening and healing prayer over time! As God heals you, you will be even more able to help others!

After completing these steps, you will be ready to come alongside others as they go through the steps as well. Encourage the women you are discipling to spend quiet time with God, journaling their insights and thoughts from the guiding questions for the healing process. You can be of help to them as you discuss their insights, particularly in the area of forgiveness. Some helpful verses on forgiveness and making amends are Matthew 5:23-24,43-48; 18:21-35; Mark 11:25; and Luke 17:3-4. Spend time meditating and journaling notes about these Scriptures so that you are prepared when you meet with the women you disciple.

After several discipleship meetings with a woman, you may conclude that she has some needs that are beyond your expertise and that require professional counseling. You may notice that even after healing prayer, she still has many unresolved issues or mental health needs. Although you might continue to support her in discipleship, she may need simultaneous professional help or support-group involvement. Your pastor may be a good source for trustworthy referrals.

LEARNING THE ROUTE BY HEART

Becoming a disciple is clearly a process—a journey of walking in His power while discipling other women to follow Jesus. As you memorize your verse for the next session ask God to help you rely more on His power for your transformation and for transformation for the women you disciple.

> ## Topic: Relationship with Jesus
> *We proclaim him, admonishing and teaching everyone with all wisdom, so that we may present everyone perfect in Christ. To this end I labor, struggling with all his energy, which so powerfully works in me.*
>
> (COLOSSIANS 1:28-29)

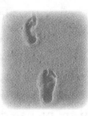

Next Steps on the Journey

Complete these items before the next meeting:

- Read and complete "Session 7: The Process of Discipling Others."
- Memorize Colossians 1:28-29 and review the verses from previous sessions.
- Read Acts 17-19 and come prepared to share a recent devotional highlight from your journal.
- Be prepared to share a truth that God revealed to you during your healing prayer time.
- Consider women whom God has brought your way who need a gentle and tender hand because of wounds they have experienced. How could you reach out to them?

THE PROCESS OF DISCIPLING OTHERS

"HOW IS TRANSFORMATION EVIDENT IN THE LIFE OF A NEW DISCIPLE?

We proclaim him, admonishing and teaching everyone with all
wisdom, so that we may present everyone perfect in Christ.
To this end I labor, struggling with all his energy,
which so powerfully works in me.
(COLOSSIANS 1:28-29)

As we learned in the last session, our disciplemaking role involves bringing women to Jesus for healing. Listening and healing prayer can be an integral part of their (and our) healing. Clearly, becoming a disciple is not an event but a journey of development, imitating Christ by walking with Him in His power. The spiritual process involves stages similar to our physical development. The changes begin in our heart and are exercised as our speech, behavior, priorities, and actions gradually become more aligned with Jesus. This process is transformation.

We invite you to learn the skill of helping new disciples discover the vital ingredients that lead to transformation in Jesus Christ.

MY DAILY JOURNEY

In your journal, write out thoughts from your devotional times: what you are learning about God or yourself, how these truths can help you grow deeper in relationship with Him, and how you can demonstrate His love to others.

OUR JOURNEY TOGETHER

In your group:

- Share a recent highlight from your personal devotional times.
- Review together your memory verse, Colossians 1:28-29.
- Tell about a truth God revealed to you during your healing times of prayer.
- Relay some ways in which you have reached out to women who need a gentle and tender hand because of woundedness. (Please remember confidentiality in sharing. Withhold names and mention only the general situation in which you reached out; no specific identifying details, please.)

Reflections from the Heart of a Discipler

"Mentoring and Mothering," by Gigi Busa

I often compare discipling to parenting. Spiritual moms need to know what to expect in their spiritual child's first year. To watch a new believer discover for the first time how much God loves her is a thrill for me. I am as proud as a new mom, watching her grow from a new believer into a mature, godly woman and eventually taking her place as a disciplemaker.

When a baby comes into the world, her mom feeds her every two hours or so and changes her diaper whenever needed. The infant is utterly dependent on her mom to meet every need. What would happen if instead Mom placed her child in the nursery, expecting her infant to care for herself?

On a spiritual level, this kind of neglect sometimes does happen. A woman may accept Jesus as Savior, be prayed with, and be sent on her way as though the process were complete. However, salvation is just the start of the process of healthy growth that should take place in her life. This new believer has no idea how to nurture herself. She'll have many questions as she reads the Word and listens to the preaching. But whom can she ask? She probably wants to follow Jesus, but she may struggle with sin and doubts. She wonders if any other believer has a past to rival her own history. After a few weeks, she might decide, *I must not be the kind of woman God wants* and stops going to church and falls away from Jesus all together.

What this new Christian needs is a spiritual mom! She needs someone to disciple her. Just as a toddler learns by imitating her mom, a new believer learns by following the example of her discipler. The discipler's role is to model the Christian life. My "spiritual mom" and I had our devotional times together and I learned to "drink the milk of the Scripture." She taught me to "speak" to my Father as I learned to pray in conversations with Him. I learned to "walk" like a Christian as she helped me to apply Scripture to my life. Like a toddler, I often fell down as I learned to walk. I cried in embarrassment, but she lovingly picked me up and led me back to my Father in confession. There was no shaming — only gentle affirmation to press on. She did not expect me, a baby Christian, to act like a mature believer. In this environment of grace, I experienced the freedom to ask about many topics that were not part of the discipleship study plan.

In addition to life-to-life time, my "mom" involved me in Bible study groups and proudly introduced me to her friends. She realized that as vital as a spiritual mom is to a spiritual child's life, it takes a whole church to raise a child!

After this stage, my spiritual mom helped me to see that it was time to learn to eat solid food — the meat of the Word — and grow to a deeper level of commitment to Jesus. I began to take responsibility to serve. It was time for me to apprentice in teaching and discipling other women. It took prodding to get me out of the comfortable nest she had built for me.

Deuteronomy 32:11 says, "Like an eagle that stirs up its nest and hovers over its young, that spreads its wings to catch them and carries them on its pinions." My spiritual mother confidently said, "You can do this. I will be praying for you." She was aware of the tendency some of us moms have to over protect our children when they reach their teens. She didn't want to keep me dependent on her; she wanted me to learn my own "God lessons" as she released me from the nest but stayed nearby to give me ongoing, consistent encouragement.

Now that I have spiritual children of my own, I realize that as natural parents do, we disciplers experience heartache when our spiritual children rebel. After investing a lot of time and love in several women, they got sidetracked from the path and went over cliffs of materialism, addiction, and self-absorption. I prayed; I exhorted; I cried. I am grieved to see the ripple effect of sin on their families' lives. I pray often for these wandering children.

When you give your life away for the Lord, there will be heartache; some children may wander for a season. But the joy you will experience in watching others complete their journey of discipleship far outweighs the grief.

—————————————

THE TRAVEL GUIDE

From Gigi's story, you can see that there are common steps in our transformation, taking people from new believers to mature Christians. Just as you have experienced transformation in your life, there is the special joy in seeing this process in the lives of the women you are discipling. Third John 4 expresses it so well: "I have no greater joy than to hear that my children are walking in the truth."

Let's see what God's Word says about this process of transformation.

1. The following verses use the word *transform*. What observations can you make from these verses regarding the change process? How can this help you influence the women you are discipling?

   a. Romans 12:1-3

   b. 2 Corinthians 3:18

2. Read 1 Thessalonians chapters 1–3. What observations did Paul, Silas, and Timothy make about the changes they saw in these new disciples? How did these life changes impact others?

3. It is impossible to become a discipler without personal life change. How do the following passages describe this transformation?

   a. Ephesians 4:22-24

   b. Colossians 3:9-10

   c. 1 Peter 1:14-16

4. It's important to share with the women you are discipling how God is at work in your life. What examples of personal spiritual transformation could you share? Consider such things as developing a hunger for God's Word or overcoming a habit that had inhibited you in your Christian walk.

5. As you think of your own ongoing transformation, what benefits have you experienced that made the challenges of growing and changing worth it? Which ones of these would offer the most encouragement to the women you are discipling?

6. Read Hebrews 12:1-3 and 1 Corinthians 9:24-27. Think back to session 5, where you thought about these verses in the context of spiritual disciplines. How would you explain to the person you are discipling the importance of spiritual discipline in the process of transformation?

7. What are some of the vital ingredients for spiritual growth as described in the following Scriptures? Think about how you would share these key points with the women you are discipling.

   a. Proverbs 27:17

   b. John 14:21

c. 2 Corinthians 12:9-10

d. Ephesians 3:16

e. Hebrews 12:11

8. Have any of these essential ingredients for transformation been especially significant in your spiritual growth? If so, how? Consider sharing these things with your disciple.

9. It can be helpful to see where the person you are discipling falls in the different stages of spiritual maturity. As you read across the following chart, notice the progression of growth from one phase of growth to the next phase. As you read vertically, notice how each phase is described.

PHASES OF TRANSFORMATION IN THE DISCIPLING PROCESS

PHASE 1 A SEEKER	PHASE 2 A DISCIPLE	PHASE 3 DISCIPLER OF OTHERS	PHASE 4 A FRUITFUL LEADER
Jesus said, "Come and see" John 1:38-39	Jesus said, "Come, follow Me" Mark 1:17	Jesus said, " Come and be with Me" Mark 3:13; John 13:34-35	Jesus said, "Remain in Me" John 15:7-8; Matthew 28:18-20
Choose to come	Choose to follow Him	Enjoy His presence and His relationship	Conform to His image
Learn who Jesus is	Learn about Jesus	Learn His passion	Follow His vision and learn His mission
Allow Jesus to change your life from the inside out	Experience life change by following Jesus	Experience Jesus loving others through you	Experience the joy of your children walking the truth see 3 John 3
Becoming a believer	Becoming an established disciple	Becoming a discipler of others	Becoming a fruitful leader

Based on the chart, in what phase of maturity do the women you are discipling seem to be?

When a disciple takes the next steps to follow Jesus, transformation begins to happen. The role of a disciplemaker is to encourage and help equip a disciple to take the next step. Each step she takes in following Christ leads one step closer to being transformed into His image.

Show the chart to your disciple. Ask her where she sees herself in this process, and discuss what the next step might be for her growth and development.

10. Suppose you are meeting with two young women, Jennifer and Kristen. As you review the phases, you realize that although they have participated in Bible studies for many years, they are not investing in others' lives. What suggestions would you make to encourage them to deepen their Christian experience and their relationship with God?

11. Read the following verses from Ephesians and Philippians. For each Scripture, write a prayer asking God to work in the lives of your disciples. Use these prayers often as you intercede for the transformation of the women you are discipling.

   a. Ephesians 1:18-19

   b. Philippians 2:12-13

WRITINGS ALONG THE WAY

Speaking the Truth in Love
Even When It Hurts

by Gigi Busa

What should you do when the woman you are discipling has lost her passion for Christ?

Discipling is like parenting. Your spiritual child may wander from the path of following Christ for a time. This detour may be obvious as in willful sin or it may be obscure like in a career pursuit or a relationship that begins to take priority over Jesus.

What are signs of a cooling heart and what should your response be as a discipler?

Signs such as a lack of enthusiasm for daily time with God, inconsistent church attendance, withdrawal, and continually canceling appointments with you could be indicators of a cooling heart toward God. No one just decides to make a mess of their life. Gradual steps of decline begin to reveal a cooling heart. Revelations 2:4-5 warns the people of Ephesus that they have forsaken their first love. They were encouraged to remember the height of the love compared to where they were now, and to do the things they once did in order to follow Christ. Look at scripture like this and other scriptures, and pray together over them. There is nothing more powerful than the combination of the Word and prayer to encourage your disciple toward re-igniting her passion for Christ. Talk with her about the value of an accountability relationship and how being vulnerable with one another could empower them to live victoriously.

What should your response be if the disciple is not addressing an obvious sin?

One of the most destructive attributes is an un-teachable spirit. Underlying this is usually cherished sin, which she may be reluctant to expose.

1 Thessalonians 2:12 instructs the discipler to "urge them (the disciples) to live lives worthy of God." As a discipler you cannot neglect situations that present spiritual harm to the woman you are discipling. Your response should be to speak in a loving manner about the sin, allowing scriptures to address the issues, while praying for the Holy Spirit to change her heart. Share the truth in love with her, but take care to avoid being judgmental or using words that condemn or make her feel guilty. It is the Holy Spirit's role to convict of sin.

If you have done all this in love and have prayed for a time, waiting on the Lord to change her, and there is still no repentance on the disciple's part, it is time to take a stronger stand. Explain to her that without accountability and a teachable spirit discipleship is no longer taking place. Tell her you will continue to love her and pray for her, but that your role as her discipler has stopped by her choice. Assure her that the door is open when she decides to turn her life back over to Christ and pursue the discipleship path she has left. Meanwhile maintain a friendship with her.

These issues of discipline could be painful for both of you. Maintaining the friendship is a critical link to successfully seeing your disciple through this type of crisis. Prayer for your friend is the most powerful tool. Reminders in notes and calls will reflect God's loving care and tug on her wandering heart.

Remember though this is certainly discouraging, it is not a failure in your efforts to disciple. You are responsible TO the disciple in fulfilling your role; not FOR the disciple's wrong choices.

The final chapter remains to be seen in this person's life. There's nothing more encouraging than a wandering "child" returning to the truth. You will hear words like "I'll never forget how you continued to love me. The scriptures and God's love were a constant reminder of what I was missing,"

Meanwhile, keep your focus on God, knowing that He desires to care for and guide His precious drifting child even more than you do.

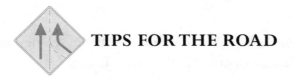

TIPS FOR THE ROAD

POLISHING A DIAMOND IN THE ROUGH

A diamond is a lovely and valuable thing. Just about everyone admires the brilliance of a diamond as it sparkles and reflects light. When a skilled jeweler cuts and polishes a diamond, it will be dazzling in its beauty as it reflects light from every angle. Let's imagine for a moment a diamond with four facets. Let each facet remind you of an aspect of the image of Jesus that God is polishing in your disciple through transformation.

- **Reflection:** Just as a diamond reflects light, it is also important that your disciple's life reflect the joy of Christ as she reaches out to share Him with others. Let's call this facet "Evangelize."
- **Strength:** Diamonds are known for their durability. In a Christian's "polishing" process, it is an intentional reliance on God's Word that provides spiritual strength and durability. Call this facet "Establish."
- **Value:** Diamonds have intrinsic value. In the same way (only much more!), your disciple is valued in God's eyes, created with a unique purpose. God longs to show her what He has in mind for her life as He provides opportunities for her growth. This facet can be called "Equip."
- **Symbol:** Diamonds are forever; they are a symbol of commitment. God's

desire for us and our disciples is that we make a lifetime commitment to walk with Christ as His ambassadors. Call this facet "Engage."

You may want to share this illustration with the women you are discipling to help them recognize and pursue the various aspects of transformation that are true in the lives of Jesus' disciples.

LEARNING THE ROUTE BY HEART

The Bible is God's manual directing you to the nourishment and guidance you need for your journey with the living Christ. As you memorize the verse for the next session, pray that you will develop a lifestyle that abides in His Word and that multiplies in the lives of the women you disciple.

Topic: The Importance of the Word

All Scripture is God-breathed and is useful for teaching, rebuking, correcting and training in righteousness, so that the man of God may be thoroughly equipped for every good work.

(2 TIMOTHY 3:16-17)

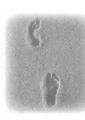

Next Steps on the Journey

Complete these items before the next meeting:
- Read and complete "Session 8: Relying on the Guide Book."
- Memorize 2 Timothy 3:16-17 and review the verses from previous sessions.
- Read Acts 20-22 and come prepared to share a recent devotional highlight from your journal.
- Reflect on what significant life changes you have made as a result of growing in Christ. Also think about what evidences of life change you see in the women you are discipling.

RELYING ON THE GUIDE BOOK

"HOW CAN I EFFECTIVELY USE GOD'S WORD TO DISCIPLE OTHERS?"

All Scripture is God-breathed and is useful for teaching, rebuking, correcting and training in righteousness, so that the man of God may be thoroughly equipped for every good work.
(2 TIMOTHY 3:16-17)

In the last session, you were reminded that discipleship is a process of reflecting more clearly the image of Jesus Christ. The growth of godly character in your life and in the lives of the women you disciple will become increasingly evident as you allow the Holy Spirit to control your lives instead of yielding to worldly desires.

It's possible even for believers to be influenced by the world's way of thinking. If you allow the world's values to diminish your desire to disciple others or sway your thinking, you could end up like the women described in 2 Timothy 3:6-7. These women had a desire to learn but were weak-willed and never acknowledged the truth.

To avoid these pitfalls, make it your aim to be skilled in handling the Word of God. Allow the Bible to be the foundation of your life, the plumb line for your daily thoughts, words, and actions.

We invite you to discover the vast resource God's Word is for your life and the lives of the women you disciple.

MY DAILY JOURNEY

In your journal, write out thoughts from your devotional times: what you are learning about God or yourself, how these truths can help you grow deeper in your relationship with Him, and how you can demonstrate His love to others.

OUR JOURNEY TOGETHER

In your group:

- Share a recent highlight from your personal devotional times.
- Review together your memory verse, 2 Timothy 3:16-17.
- Share with the group a new insight or lesson you learned about the value of knowing and using God's Word.

Reflections from the Heart of a Discipler

"Establish My Footsteps in Your Word," by Diane Manchester

Growing up, my values were molded by the world. In fact, when I debated a Christian friend who said that she believed and followed all that was in the Bible, I later said to myself and other unbelieving friends, "To believe the whole Bible is like intellectual suicide!"

How I now cringe to think that I ever said those words. My pride in my own intellectualism led me to think that I could reason and handle pretty much anything life could hurl at me.

In my late twenties and early thirties, life hurled three extreme physical traumas at me: a grisly skiing accident that paralyzed me in one of my legs; a ruptured tubal pregnancy, from which I almost died; and a painful herniated disk in my lower back. I credited my survival to my own fortitude and high pain tolerance, until God began opening my eyes to His hand in my life.

My knees finally buckled when my marriage went into a tailspin. After two years of secular counseling, my husband and I separated. In the crisis that followed, I realized that I had finally reached the limit of my own resources. I envisioned myself trudging through a dark tunnel with no end in sight. As a last resort, I began attending church with my preschool daughters. I even bought a used Bible for a dollar! In the evenings, rather than lying on the floor and crying, I read the Gospels. Before long, I realized that I had never read anything so beautiful. The unconditional love of Jesus and His concern for individuals brought hope to my heart. I related to the apostle Paul's conversion, that "there fell from his eyes something like scales" (Acts 9:18, NASB). Through His Word, He showed me my need for His salvation and His solutions for my life. No longer blind, I saw His compassion and how in the past He had protected me from my own foolishness.

When I began meeting with another woman for one-to-one discipleship, I started becoming a "tree firmly planted by streams of water" (Psalm 1:3). Yet early in my budding faith in Christ, I could not understand people who said that they loved the Lord. Not only that, when I first read Psalm 119, I was amazed at the many ways the psalmist could say, "I love Your law!" and he also showed great passion for God's precepts, statutes, commandments, ways, and Word! My pride and independent spirit kept me from receiving God's love for me.

Then, when I was about a year old in my faith, the Holy Spirit moved me to surrender my life to God and allow Him to use me as He saw best. At that point, God supernaturally touched my heart. I experienced the truth of Galatians 2:20, "I no longer live but Christ lives in me." I had an unquenchable thirst for God's Word. As I studied Scripture, I was drawn to and memorized Psalm 119:11, "Your word I have treasured in my heart" (NASB).

As I memorized Scripture, I was drawn back into Psalm 119. From that chapter, I discovered verse 67: "Before I was afflicted I went astray, but now I keep Your word." I realized that verse pretty much summed up my journey. God had used my traumas to draw me to Himself and to His Word. Rather than letting me go astray, He continues to "establish my footsteps in [His] word" (Psalm 119:133, NASB). Though far from perfection, my life, values, and decisions are now molded by Christ and His words. And, by the way, God restored our marriage!

———————————————

THE TRAVEL GUIDE

As you read Diane's story, did you notice how the Word became not only the foundation of her life but also a "treasure" for her? By modeling a life of devotion and obedience to God's Word you, too, can experience His power through you to impart this same passion to the women you are discipling. These women will be able to catch this same vision of using the Bible as their primary resource for all of life's decisions. They will be able to trust God's Word for every area of life and for every relationship they encounter.

As you go through this session, pay close attention to how you can use the authority and power of Scripture to disciple women so they, too, will be able to establish their lives on His truth and enjoy intimacy with Him. And by growing in intimacy with the Lord and applying these scriptural truths, they will gain passion to influence future generations to follow Jesus.

1. The most important thing for someone you are discipling to understand about God's Word is that she can trust it. Being confident in the validity of the Scriptures is crucial for spiritual growth. Look up the following Scriptures and summarize your conclusions about the nature of the Word — its authority, accuracy, sufficiency, and purposes.

SCRIPTURE	NATURE OF GOD'S WORD	GOD'S PURPOSES
2 Timothy 3:14-17		
2 Peter 1:20-21		
Isaiah 55:11		
Hebrews 4:12		
Matthew 4:1-11		

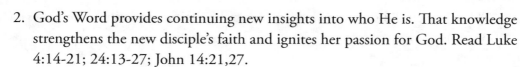

2. God's Word provides continuing new insights into who He is. That knowledge strengthens the new disciple's faith and ignites her passion for God. Read Luke 4:14-21; 24:13-27; John 14:21,27.

a. How does Scripture, both Old and New Testaments, reveal the Lord Jesus Christ?

b. According to the Luke 24 passage, how was the two disciples' knowledge about Jesus incomplete?

c. Describe a misconception you had about Jesus Christ and how Scripture brought new light to your thinking.

d. What words are used to demonstrate what God did in the disciples' hearts as Jesus shared the Scriptures with them (see Luke 24:32)?

e. What impact did that knowledge have on their faith and actions (see verses 33-35)?

The Bible is effective in discipling people in worship, and worship leads to a willing and obedient heart. Read Luke 1:45-55. One of the most astounding, yet concise, portraits of God's character and deeds is found in Mary's (the mother of Jesus) song of worship, often called the "Magnificat." Her words were Old Testament verses that portray God. Mary's heart-filled response demonstrates how well she knew God and appreciated the value of using the words of Scripture to worship Him.

3. How does Mary describe God?

Mary was a true worshipper of God and His humble servant. God chose to work through her to bring Jesus, the Messiah, to a waiting world. Generations would call her blessed! One of our roles as disciplers is to influence women to worship God truly through His Word. By modeling worship as you read Scriptures describing God's character and respond in praising Him, the women you disciple will come to know God better and grow in their adoration of Him. The result of deep worship is a willing spirit. The women you disciple will join Mary in saying, *"I am the Lord's servant. May it be to me as you have said"* (Luke 1:38).

The Scriptures are effective in discipling women to develop and maintain an intimate relationship with God. The *"great and foremost commandment"* is, *"Love the Lord your God with all your heart and with all your soul and with all your mind"* (Matthew 22:37). This commandment is about cultivating absolute devotion to and intimacy with God. God's Word helps us do that.

4. Read 1 John 4:16-21. How would you describe intimacy with God to a new disciple? (Include in your answer the effect intimacy with God has on your other relationships.)

5. Read John 15:9-13.

a. What did Jesus tell His disciples to do to be intimate with the Father?

b. How would you explain "abiding or remaining in the Word" to a woman you are discipling?

c. How could "remaining in the Word" impact her relationship with God and others?

Sometimes we may be tempted to use our own experiences to "teach" others, but Proverbs 3:5-6 states that we are to lean fully on God, not our own understanding. Other times we may think we have just the right Christian book to recommend. Stories and books may be helpful, but they don't compare with using the powerful Word of God.

The role of a discipler is to point new disciples to Jesus and His Word. Psalm 119:24 says, *"Your words are my counselors."* Your counsel and feedback should stem from the Word. Encourage and help your new disciple to look up verses where she will find true guidance, receive help in asking forgiveness for sin, and develop deep conviction for using God's Word.

6. Suppose that "Gina," a woman you are discipling, confides in you that her husband is verbally abusing her. She is very discouraged, feels alone and unloved, and doesn't know what to believe about herself. How could you use God's Word with Gina to help her discover God's deep love for her and encourage her in her intimacy with Him, despite her husband's negative input? What verses or passages would you point her to?

God's Word will impact future generations through the women you disciple.

7. Read 2 Timothy 2:15, 2 Timothy 4:1-2, Romans 10:8-17, and 1 Corinthians 15:3-7.

   a. Keeping in mind that many unbelievers may never open a Bible on their own, why is it important for you to teach your disciple that God can use her to share the truth of His Word with people she knows who don't know Him yet?

b. Have you ever shared Scripture with an unbeliever? Describe that experience to your disciple. Tell her what you did and how the other person responded.

Encourage a woman you are discipling to write out her testimony so she can have it ready to share with someone who does not yet know Christ. Help her think through the story of her spiritual journey and suggest ways she could weave appropriate Scriptures into it to create an engaging spiritual conversation. Share verses that have been instrumental in your own journey with Christ. Pray together and ask God for an opening for your friend to share her story with an unbeliever.

8. How can Isaiah 55:11 persuade you and your disciple to continue sharing Scripture regardless of others' responses?

WRITINGS ALONG THE WAY

Speaking God's Language

by Joni Eareckson Tada[1]

E. M. Bounds was known for his extraordinary prayer life. He once testified, "The Word of God is the fulcrum upon which the lever of prayer is placed, and by which things are mightily moved. God has committed Himself, His purpose, and His promise to prayer. His Word becomes the basis, the inspiration of our praying, and there are circumstances under which by importunate prayer, we may obtain an . . . enlargement of His promises."

I will never forget the time I received an "enlargement of His promises" from praying Scripture. It was in the early 1980s, not long after the honeymoon was over for two newlyweds: Ken and me. I learned that my new husband preferred to spend Monday nights in front of the TV with chips, salsa, and the NFL rather than being my hands to write out my Bible study for me. Horrors, I thought—he's not a man of the Word!

I was itching to change my husband, but my nagging and scolding only made things worse.

Feeling like a martyr, I sought help in God's Word and stumbled across these words in Philippians 2:3-4: "Do nothing out of selfish ambition or vain conceit, but in humility consider others better than yourselves. Each of you should look not only to your own interests, but also to the interests of others."

Yikes, that's me, I thought. I've wanted Ken to change for selfish reasons—so that he'll meet my expectations. And to be honest, I don't consider him "better than myself." I feel I'm the one in the right. I feel I've got it spiritually together, not him.

Convicted. These verses catapulted me into a major prayer advance for Ken. I sincerely wanted to follow God's Word and have humility of mind, as well as to regard Ken as better than I. How could I look out for his interests? I feverishly flipped through Scripture until I found the perfect passage to pray for my husband.

Who may ascend the hill of the LORD? Who may stand in his holy place? He who has clean hands and a pure heart, who does not lift up his soul to an idol or swear by what is false. He will receive blessing from the LORD and vindication from God his Savior. Such is the generation of those who seek him, who seek your face, O God of Jacob. Selah. Lift up your heads, O you gates; be lifted up, you ancient doors, that the King of glory may come in. Who is this King of glory? The LORD strong and mighty, the LORD mighty in battle. (Psalm 24:3-8)

I'd spend evenings in our bedroom, praying, "Lord, You want Ken to stand in Your holy place, to have clean hands and a pure heart. May You cause him to lift up his soul to You and receive Your blessing. May he seek Your face. Lift up the gates of Ken's heart that You, the King of glory, might come in! Lord, say to him, 'I, the King of glory, will come in and rule your life. I, the Lord, strong and mighty.'"

I can't tell you how many times I prayed this way. But now, years later, it's clear that Christ sits on the throne of my husband's heart. (He's in the process of memorizing the entire Sermon on the Mount; I didn't put him up to it—really!) Something else is clear: Ken still loves Monday Night Football. What has changed is that so do I! And I've found other "hands" to help me write out my Bible studies on other evenings.

I began praying Psalm 24 over my husband, believing that God would change him, but God did much more. He changed me. It was, as E. M. Bounds would say, "an enlargement of His promises." I'm convinced that we're still feeling the repercussions of that Scripture prayer.

That's because it was based on Psalm 24 and was alive, active, and powerful, bringing about fundamental changes in me where it counted most. And in my husband, too.

TIPS FOR THE ROAD

To accurately handle the word of truth (see 2 Timothy 2:15), we must interact with Scripture in a way that sharpens our power of observation so that we can draw accurate interpretation and application. Here is an abbreviated format for inductive Bible study that you can apply to any passage of Scripture:

- **Observe the facts**, including the what, who, when, where, and how; note repeated words and key contrasts.
- **Interpret God's message to us**—what does it mean and what are the implications?
- **Seek the timeless truths**—what truths transcend the local context?
- **Formulate biblical principles**, which emerge from the timeless truths.
- **Write personal applications**, based upon the biblical principles.

Together with a woman you are discipling, practice these steps on the Emmaus road passage, Luke 24:13-27. The more you practice, the more you will see God's truth emerge for integration into your life.

LEARNING THE ROUTE BY HEART

God loves ordinary people. One ordinary woman who loves and obeys God will impact the people in her circle of influence, but she can also have an extraordinary impact upon society and even the world! As you memorize your verse for the next session, allow the Lord to use you in the lives of the women in your world who will in turn influence their world for Christ.

Topic: The Value of Each Individual

The least of you will become a thousand, the smallest a mighty nation.
I am the LORD; in its time I will do this swiftly.
(ISAIAH 60:22)

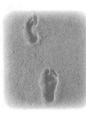

Next Steps on the Journey

Complete these items before the next meeting:

* Read and complete "Session 9: Bringing Others Along."
* Memorize Isaiah 60:22 and review the verses from previous sessions.
* Read Acts 23-25 and come prepared to share a recent devotional highlight from your journal.
* Help a woman you are discipling write out her spiritual journey conversation to introduce others to Christ.
* Work with your disciple on the inductive study you learned about in Tips for the Road on page 134.
* In your personal prayer times, pray Scripture, letting God's Word guide your prayer.

BRINGING OTHERS ALONG

"WHAT IS THE VALUE OF ONE WOMAN?

The least of you will become a thousand, the smallest a mighty
nation. I am the LORD; in its time I will do this swiftly.
(ISAIAH 60:22)

As we saw in session 8, God's Word is our source for knowing Him and developing our intimacy with Him. As we share His Word with others, we multiply His impact through the women we disciple, to the women *they* disciple, and then to generations beyond!

Even though there are more than six billion people living on our planet, God considers every single one incredibly valuable. Although we often see masses of people, He sees individuals. While we often look at people in terms of what they can do for us, He cares for every person, no matter how ordinary. He cares for both popular and obscure people. He sees both the talented and the simple. Whether least or greatest, to God each person has intrinsic value.

We invite you to grasp God's view of your value and potential impact as you commit to investing in others.

MY DAILY JOURNEY

In your journal, write out thoughts from your devotional times: what you are learning about God or yourself, how these truths can help you grow deeper in relationship with Him, and how you can demonstrate His love to others.

OUR JOURNEY TOGETHER

In your group:

- Share a recent highlight from your personal devotional times.
- Review together your memory verse, Isaiah 60:22.
- Share highlights from your Tips for the Road inductive study.

Reflections from the Heart of a Discipler

"An Ordinary Woman," by Ruth Fobes

Beth was an ordinary, down-to-earth woman who walked by faith and loved life. Her love and commitment to the Lord radiated to hundreds of women around the world as she gave her life to teach, model for, and train women so that they would in turn do the same for others. Beth expressed in her testimony: My biggest verse in the Bible to me is Isaiah 43:4: *Because you are precious in my eyes, you are honored, and I love you; therefore I will give people in your place and nations in exchange for your life.* (Berkeley) I'm very delighted to spend the rest of my life, however long it is, cooperating with God and His plan to carry out this promise for me."

Her life exemplified this Scripture.

I was one of the women privileged to be ministered to by Beth, for which I'm forever grateful. She shared her life in Jesus with me in such a way that I caught her vision and wanted to share my life in Him with others. She prayed with me and for me and taught me to use a prayer list. Her coaching planted within me a deep love for personal Bible study. She was an encourager and an exhorter whose desire to grow in her knowledge and trust of the Lord blessed me. She taught me by example to listen to the small still voice of the Holy Spirit through the gentle and gracious guidance of the Scriptures.

After years of giving her life away in ministering to women, she was diagnosed with Alzheimer's disease. I felt sad about this and had lots of questions. Her life had been so valuable before. What was her value now? And, most important, how did God value her?

Mary Zuwerink, Beth's sister, tells in her self-published book *She Shall Flourish* her perspective on how God had kingdom plans for this ordinary godly woman, even during her thirteen years with Alzheimer's.

The Lord had work for her to do, ministry for her to accomplish. That divinely chosen work, prepared in advance for her to do as an Alzheimer's patient, was a ministry of intercession. The ministry she faithfully performed until God released her from this life.

Prayer had always been a spiritual discipline that Beth had practiced. Even after she was placed in care, she worked on those prayer lists. In fact, updating them was the last intentional, rational thing she was able to do. Prayer was part of the very essence of Beth. I believe this active, faithful prayer life never ceased until she was taken into glory.[1]

She lived her life out fully and in full submission to the Father's purposes for her. Her body decayed on the altar of God's will, but her spirit — her regenerated, Spirit-filled essence — remained alive and active in His service. Through Beth's spirit and the spirit of God within her, she ministered to those around her, bearing fruit in old age. As the nurses and aides would care for her bodily needs, they would talk to her. On a daily basis they would share their lives. There was trouble at home. There were financial needs. For Beth, there was work to do, prayers to pray. She did not even need language. She did not need intellectual understanding. Her spirit perceived the need and interceded through the power of the Holy Spirit abiding in her. He helped her in her weakness, interceding for her in ways that went beyond words. By this means she ministered to, interceded for, and touched an untold number of lives.

I know Beth prayed for me, too, and her prayers live on in my life, which continues to encourage me. God used this ordinary woman to reach women all over the world for His glory. Her passion to see women discipled through Christ's love so they would reach out to their worlds in discipling others keeps on giving from one generation to another.

———————————————

THE TRAVEL GUIDE

Like Beth, most of us are also quite ordinary women. Status or influence in society, though highly regarded by the world, has no merit in the value God places on each of us. He values and cares for every person, and knows us better than we even know ourselves. The Lord sees our individual potential and significance. Scripture assures us He has created each person in His own image and has designed us to fulfill His specific purpose through the power of His Spirit that will bring Him great glory.

The perspective Jesus demonstrates on the value of an individual is one we too should emulate in our relationships with the women we disciple and all we meet on our life journey.

1. In the story you just read, how did God use this ordinary woman in an extraordinary way?

2. Read the following verses and note what place people have with God.

   a. Psalm 8:3-8

   b. Isaiah 43:4

c. 2 Peter 3:9

3. God is relational. He not only relates to groups of people, nations, and clans but also to individuals. Scripture reveals a God who longs to relate to each person individually. How do the following verses demonstrate God's involvement and love for individual people?

a. 2 Chronicles 16:9

b. Jeremiah 32:19

c. Hebrews 12:5-11

4. God is intimately familiar with each one of us. How is His knowledge and love of each person demonstrated in the following verses? As you read these Scriptures, reflect on the story of Beth and imagine how God viewed her.

a. 1 Samuel 16:7

b. Psalm 139:1-6

c. Psalm 139:13-18

d. Luke 12:6-7

e. Ephesians 2:8-10

God sees the potential and significance of each individual.

5. Take a moment to imagine how you could relate to and love individuals who are not popular or especially talented. Think of someone you know. As you think of how God values that person, consider what changes you need to make in your own attitude and behavior. Record your thoughts here.

6. Think about the lives of the following Bible characters. What contributions did each make? What influence did each have? How was each one ordinary?

   a. Joseph (see Genesis 37–47)

   b. Rahab (see Joshua 2; 6:23; Matthew 1:5; Hebrews 11:31)

c. Lydia (see Acts 16:11-40)

7. Scripture often surprises us with God's use of the common person. How do these verses exemplify the value of each person and God's desire to include people who are not highly regarded by the world's standards?

a. 1 Corinthians 1:26-29

b. 1 Corinthians 12:14-26

c. 2 Corinthians 4:7

8. Think about yourself. How are you ordinary? In spite of your ordinariness (or perhaps even because of it!), how has God shown how much He values you? How has He chosen to use you to demonstrate His love to others?

> You can't really love other people well unless you are at home in your own soul. You will simply be too afraid. We don't have to go through life using all our energy to hide our hearts and protect ourselves. We can walk in the fire of a difficult conflict or situation and not be consumed. We can love others with real abandonment. We can trust God who has nail prints in His hands.
> —Paula Rinehart, *Strong Women, Soft Hearts*

9. The way Jesus treated people demonstrated His value for ordinary individuals. Complete the following chart to help you reflect on two people whose lives Jesus touched.

Person	How Jesus demonstrated the worth of the individual	The result of His personal attention
Zacchaeus (see Luke 19:1-10)		
Woman at the well (see John 4:4-30,39-42)		

10. Name some "ordinary" people in your life whom God might want you to notice and become more involved with.

WRITINGS ALONG THE WAY

The Importance of Every Individual

by Lorne Sanny[2]

Imagine for a moment that you own a valuable treasure. You would, of course, value it highly. And suppose that obtaining this treasure had cost you very dearly. You'd cherish it all the more. And suppose you knew that in the future your treasure would become even greater in its beauty and worth. You would, if possible, consider it more precious still. You are all this, and more, to God.

Let's think a moment, about you. The Bible admonishes each of us, "Do not think of yourself more highly than you ought, but rather think of yourself with sober judgment, in accordance with the measure of faith God has given you" (Romans 12:3). Discussing the importance of every individual—your importance—is necessary because many of us just don't think with sober judgment about ourselves. It seems we fluctuate from one extreme to another.

Maybe you feel uncomfortable down inside, insecure or fearful or frustrated. You smile as you pass by others and you laugh with your friends, but the smile on your face may hide a tear in your heart. Sometimes, as you know, outward bravado simply masks inner insecurity.

God is interested in individuals. Jesus was coming into Jericho. The streets were jammed with people so a short man named Zacchaeus climbed a tree to see him. When Jesus came by, of all the people there, he picked out this one little guy and said, "Come down, Zacchaeus, I'm coming to your house today!" That is true also for us. The Lord asks for you, because you're important to him.

Three reasons why you're important to God:

1. YOU'RE CREATED IN THE IMAGE OF GOD.

"God said, 'Let us make man in our image, in our likeness.' So God created man in his own image, in the image of God he created him; male and female he created them" (Genesis 1:26-27).

Who are you? You're a being created in God's image. That means first that you have a unique, recognizable personality. You're valuable. In fact, one individual is worth more than the whole earth. Jesus said, "What good is it for a man to gain the whole world, yet forfeit his soul? Or what can a man give in exchange for his soul?" (Mark 8:36-37).

2. YOU'RE IMPORTANT BECAUSE OF WHAT YOU COST.

You cost God the best heaven had. Have you seen Christ on the cross for you? That's what you cost God, and you are valuable to God by virtue of that cost. Peter wrote, "It was not with perishable things such as silver or gold that you were redeemed from the empty way of life handed down to you from your forefathers, but with the precious blood of Christ, a lamb without blemish or defect" (1 Peter 1:18-19).

3. YOU'RE IMPORTANT BECAUSE OF WHAT YOU CAN BECOME.

This occurs under the transforming power of the Holy Spirit. Jesus saw in Simon what he could become under the Holy Spirit's power: You are Simon; you will be Peter. You're a small stone; you'll be a big rock. You're a moral coward now; you'll be courageous. You're unreliable and unstable; you'll be stable and steady. We see what Jesus meant when Peter abjectly denied his Lord but later preached Christ boldly.

 TIPS FOR THE ROAD

What should you do when you are tempted to ignore the individuals who are not popular or especially talented? Think of some of the people you just read about.

Here are some ideas that may help you overcome your temptation to overlook these individuals:

Pray for them

- Prayer brings people together. God does amazing things in your heart when you pray for others.
- Pray Scripture into those people's lives.

Show love and acts of kindness

- In session 2, along with the Great Commission, you studied the Great Commandment, John 13:34-35: "Love one another as I have loved you." Reflect on how you answered question 9 in session 2: How could you express the Great Commandment as you live out the Great Commission?
- A genuine way to show love is through acts of kindness. What acts of kindness could you do to show love?

Don't compare

- We live in a culture in which we face constant comparisons, especially among women. But 2 Corinthians 10:12 warns us against comparing: "We dare not classify or compare ourselves with one another. Those that do are not wise."

Envision a future for her

- What would you like to see God do in and through her life? As you answer this question, think back on Session 1, The Discipling Vision.

Be patient

- Patience is one of the fruits of the Spirit, as expressed in Galatians 5:22. Allow the Spirit of God to work in your heart to give you this attribute of the Spirit.

Be creative

- Ask the Lord for creativity and ideas in how to get to know one another. Think of fun things you both might enjoy doing together. Shared experiences build memories and deepen relationships.

Persevere

- Ask the Lord for strength to keep going. Don't give up.
- Pray Philippians 4:13, "I can do everything through him who gives me strength."

LEARNING THE ROUTE BY HEART

Leaving a trail for others to follow is leaving a spiritual legacy, which is eternal! As you memorize your verse for the next session, pray about the link you and the women you disciple will be to multitudes of women many years from now.

Topic: Spiritual Generations

"And the things you have heard me say in the presence of many witnesses entrust to reliable men who will also be qualified to teach others."

(2 TIMOTHY 2:2)

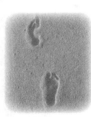

Next Steps on the Journey

Complete these items before the next meeting:

- Read and complete "Session 10: Leaving a Trail for Others to Follow."
- Memorize 2 Timothy 2:2 and review the verses from previous sessions.
- Read Acts 26-28 and come prepared to share a recent devotional highlight from your journal.
- Share what you have learned about the value of one woman.

LEAVING A TRAIL FOR OTHERS TO FOLLOW

"How can I leave a spiritual legacy?"

*The things you have heard me say in the presence of many witnesses
entrust to reliable men who will also be qualified to teach others.*
(2 Timothy 2:2)

In the previous session, we focused on the amazing truth that God cares for each of us as unique individuals who have the ability to impact the world for Jesus Christ over generations. In this session, we will focus on our role in bringing forth new life. For some of us, bringing forth new life is an experience we've had as we've given birth to or adopted children. But regardless of whether we have our own families or not, God calls all women to give spiritual birth and raise new generations of believers through discipleship. God's passion is to bring all people to Him through Jesus. The gospel is a generational trust God has placed in your heart. It is your legacy to be passed through your spiritual descendants. This legacy is the heart of the Great Commission.

We invite you to learn how you will be a link in this special legacy as you make disciples who will pass this eternal treasure on to other women.

MY DAILY JOURNEY

In your journal, write out thoughts from your devotional times: what you are learning about God or yourself, how these truths can help you grow deeper in relationship with Him, and how you can demonstrate His love to others.

OUR JOURNEY TOGETHER

In your group:

- Share a recent highlight from your personal devotional times.
- Review together your memory verse, 2 Timothy 2:2.
- Express your thoughts about your value in God's eyes.

Reflections from the Heart of a Discipler

"Where Will the Seeds Blow?" by Ruth Fobes and Gigi Busa (dedicated to Chris Kemmerer)

Two young Christian women, Ruth and Chris, were traveling cross-country to a conference and decided to redeem the long hours of driving time in prayer, specifically asking God to use their lives to influence future generations of disciples. Although their lives changed when they married and started their families, they persisted in that prayer and continued to disciple women. Over the years, God answered their prayer again and again, but in one particular way the prayer was answered for both of them through a single person.

Several years after that trip, Chris discipled a college student, Elaine, who later married and moved to New England, where her husband pastored a small church. Elaine discipled Gigi, a new believer, who in turn began to disciple

152

others, resulting in five spiritual generations at that church: Elaine, Gigi, Michelle, Christine, and Kristen (and more to come!).

Of course, the spiritual generations did not begin with Elaine; they were birthed in the prayer of those two young women, Ruth and Chris. When Ruth moved to the East Coast, she met Gigi. Imagine their shared surprise and delight when, after comparing stories, the two of them discovered that Gigi was one of Chris' spiritual grandchildren! Chris and Ruth had prayed for spiritual generations during that trip so many years ago, and Ruth was now getting to meet "an answer" to those prayers!

Ruth arranged for Gigi to meet her spiritual grandmother, Chris. Gigi wanted Chris to know how her influence had impacted generations of disciples in one church where Gigi served as women's ministry director. She showed Chris the women's ministry booklet she had developed, which explained how:

- Three discipleship classes were taught yearly.
- Seventeen disciplers led eight Bible studies, reaching more than eighty women.
- Five disciplers ministered to young moms and babies.
- Five disciplers planned three outreach events as well as an annual retreat.

Gigi excitedly explained to an astonished Chris how discipleship was the foundation of each facet of the women's ministry and that all the leaders had caught the vision of disciplemaking as they led their small groups. When they added up numbers, they realized that the discipling process had impacted more than two hundred women! Some disciples had moved to other churches in other states, and a few had gone to the mission field, where they continue to make disciples wherever God plants them. It was obvious that the heart and vision for disciplemaking was the life flow of the ministry God had given Gigi.

Chris's joyful tears flowed when she heard about the hundreds of transformed lives. This is Chris' spiritual legacy through just *one* of her spiritual grandchildren in just *one* church! We know God answered Chris and Ruth's prayer to influence future generations of disciples far more than they could ever imagine, but only in heaven will it be known just how many lives have been transformed.

A women's discipling ministry usually starts small, with one woman reaching out to one other woman. If after a period of six months to one year this new woman begins to disciple another woman and the first woman begins to disciple someone else, there will now be four women in the process of discipleship. If each disciple continues in this process, note how many disciples there will be after fifteen years:

- After one year, there will be two disciples.
- After two years, there will be four disciples.
- After five years, there will be thirty-two disciples.
- After ten years, there will be 1,024 disciples.
- After fifteen years, there will be 32,768 disciples.

If you have been praying for and reaching out to at least one woman during the course of this study, you have already begun the multiplication process. Continue to pray for and disciple the women God has entrusted to you; you could very well be the first link in a long chain of spiritual generations. Just imagine how many disciples could be following Jesus fifteen years from now!

In *A Legacy of Prayer*, author Jennifer Kennedy Dean wrote,

You can reach into the future through prayer this very day. You can . . . impact the world for generations to come. Consider this: As you pray for generations yet unborn, maybe one of those descendants will take the gospel to a previously un-reached corner of the world . . . Your life can impact a people of whom you have never heard, and you can be instrumental in bringing forth generations of believers from a nation you may never see.[1]

Ruth, Chris, Elaine, and Gigi all continue to disciple women. They see the value of one woman discipling another, who disciples yet another, and they continue to pray for future generations of disciples.

———————————————

THE TRAVEL GUIDE

Remember that a spiritual generation is what results when God works through one believer to birth a new generation of believers. Multiple, continuous links hold a chain together. Each person can be a link in a spiritual chain that reaches into the future. The chain creates a legacy of spiritual descendants allowing one to "become a thousand, the smallest a mighty nation" (Isaiah 60:22).

1. What do the following verses teach about spiritual generations?

   a. Genesis 17:7-10

   b. Deuteronomy 6:4-9

   c. Isaiah 44:3

The apostle Paul frequently used a family metaphor in his letters to explain the new relationships we have as followers of Christ. In Romans 4:16-17, Paul states that Abraham, who is the patriarch of the Jewish nation, also is father of the family of faith. This new faith family is made up of everyone who believes the promises of God. As part of that spiritual heritage, Paul then uses the term *children* to refer to those who believed God's promise through his ministry. Notice, for example, Galatians 4:19-20, where Paul speaks tenderly of the people he is discipling: "My dear children, for whom I am again in the pains of childbirth until Christ is formed in you, how I wish I could be with you now."

The family of faith expands through history — one person — one generation at a time.

> *The test of any work of evangelism is not what is seen at the moment but in the effectiveness with which the work continues into the next generation.*
> — Robert Coleman, *Master Plan of Evangelism*

2. Scripture often refers to multiple generations. God's design is for each generation to pass on spiritual faith lessons and a profound desire to know and obey Him. Identify the generations referred to in the following passages.

a. Psalm 78:1-6

b. Isaiah 59:21

c. 2 Timothy 2:2

Jesus is our example of praying for generations. In John 17:20, He prayed, "My prayer is not for them alone. I pray also for those who will believe in me through their message." Just think! Jesus prayed for those who would follow Him until the end of time. He was praying the truth of Psalm 102:18: "Let this be written for a future generation, that a people not yet created may praise the LORD."

3. Follow Jesus'—and Chris and Ruth's—example and ask God to give you future generations. Write your prayer here:

> *You can leave a spiritual trust that can never be stolen; squandered or lost. . . .*
> *You can store up spiritual riches and put them on deposit*
> *for generations to follow. Your prayers put spiritual riches on deposit*
> *for your descendants. As they learn to pray they will be*
> *accessing the spiritual riches you have stored up for them.*
> —Jennifer Kennedy Dean, *A Legacy of Prayer*

4. Much of Jesus' teaching about spiritual generations comes from examples of fruitfulness in nature. What do these passages teach about bearing spiritual fruit—that is, about leaving a legacy of spiritual generations?

a. Matthew 13:18-23

b. John 15:1-16

5. How could you begin to help build a spiritual legacy for women who do not have one?

6. After you've met with the women you are discipling for a few months and they are getting established in the basics of their lives with Christ, how could you begin to impart to them a vision for spiritual generations?

7. In 1 Thessalonians 2, verses 7, 8, 11, and 12, Paul compared himself to a father and mother in the way he ministered to the new believers in Corinth. What are the implications of this illustration as you think of your own ministry to others?

WRITINGS ALONG THE WAY

Motivation for a Lifetime of Disciplemaking

by Jim White[2]

Motivations to continue discipling are:

- the love of God filling our heart
- our own desire to grow
- embracing God's Word in our mind
- our longing to see God glorified

Our attempts to motivate others in the Christian life can be ineffective. We can teach and train them, but only the Holy Spirit can truly motivate them to a lifetime of discipleship and disciplemaking. A heart flooded with God's love may be the most important motivation of all. Paul wrote, "For Christ's love compels us, because we are convinced that one died for all" (2 Corinthians 5:14). If each of us knew how much God really loves us, we would never know another insecure moment. We'd be truly free to love others.

Paul longed to be personally involved in building up people as disciples, but this would also be for his own growth and encouragement. Someone who wants to grow knows he must listen and learn.

Sooner or later, all of us will go through tough times. Jeremiah was going through such a time as recorded in Jeremiah 20:7-9, and he responded this way: "I am ridiculed all day long; everyone mocks me. The word of the LORD has brought me insult and reproach all day long. But if I say, 'I will not mention him or speak any more in his name' his word is in my heart like a burning fire." The Word of God burning in our hearts will keep us going.

What can take away our motivation? One thing that will is becoming system-centered rather than God-centered. There's a fine line here. I believe a lot of people aren't making disciples because they don't have a system and they don't know what to do. But if you take structure too far, God gets pushed out of the picture.

Jesus warned us about another crippler of our motivation in Mark 4:19: "the worries of this life" that come in and choke God's Word and make it unfruitful. This anxiety means we're self-conscious rather than God-conscious or others-conscious.

Ask God to let His Holy Spirit flood your heart with His love, to show you how much He loves you so you can turn to others and love them. Make this vow to Him: "Lord, I know I'm human and I'll break this vow before tomorrow morning without your grace. But to the best of my ability for the rest of my life, I will do what I can for your glory."

And finally, ask God to send someone or some experience to get your attention whenever you begin to veer off course, so you can correct yourself before it's too late. I can't think of a better prayer than this: "Lord, on the day You return or on the day You take me home, may there never have been a day in my life when I loved You more or was obeying You more quickly than on that last day."

 TIPS FOR THE ROAD

When you are discipling, you will receive support through an accountability group with women who have the same passion for Jesus and others that you do. When Gigi began the habit of meeting one day each month with God, she invited three other women to join her. For sixteen years, their sole (and soul) purpose for meeting has been to encourage each other to become all they can be for God. They ask each other probing questions and come prepared not only to share but also to submit to each other's wisdom and counsel. They've learned the wisdom of Proverbs 27:17: "As iron sharpens iron, so one [woman] sharpens another." The group members have supported each other through crises in both family and ministry. When one of them goes through a time when she does not have the faith to believe, the others believe for her, praying for and encouraging her until she is back on her spiritual feet.

Giving your life away in discipleship will bring both joy and heartache, depending on the decisions your disciple makes along the way. Iron-sharpening sisters can be the balm for the heartache and the prodding to continue to give your life away. These are friends who stick closer than sisters and stir us on this journey of discipleship.

Who are some godly women with whom you could start an accountability group?

- Ask God whom He would have you include in your accountability group.
- Keep the number to no fewer than three and no more than five. Each of the women must commit to keep this meeting a priority in her life.
- At a minimum, meet every other month.
- Allow two to three hours for each woman to share and for the group to pray together.
- A good format for your time might include sharing concerns or joys regarding your spiritual disciplines, current goals, family needs, and any sin you are struggling with.
- Remember to keep everything that is shared confidential. Spend a good portion of your time together praying for one another.
- Be the kind of friend to your accountability sisters as you would like them to be to you.

Now that you have come this far on your journey, always keep in mind the vision and heart that Jesus has modeled for you. Ask yourself where you'd be if no one had discipled you. How would the lack of discipleship have impacted your relationship with God? At first your discipler may not have felt as though she had the time to spend with you, but she counted the cost and made the time so that you could be a link to future generations of disciples.

How will you spend your life? If you don't intentionally invest your life in the Lord's service, you will invest it somewhere else. Maybe your career will hold priority, perhaps a lovely decorated home, relationships, exercise and a healthy body, living financially secure, and the list goes on and on. A multitude of things exist in which we can invest our lives. Many pursuits are worthwhile, but none has the eternal value of discipleship. Like a rock thrown into the pond, God will cause the ripples of your life to extend far beyond your wildest dreams!

> *Unless a kernel of wheat falls to the ground and dies, it remains only a single seed. But if it dies it produces many seeds. (John 12:24)*

As we come to the close of this final session, ponder this question: How will this journey of discipleship affect your life and the lives of other women? Write your prayer of commitment to the Lord.

LEARNING THE ROUTE BY HEART

The vision of *Friends on the Journey* is expressed in 2 Timothy 2:2, the verse you memorized for this session. Paul faithfully discipled Timothy and instructed him to find reliable people who would in turn disciple others. You too have been trained and entrusted with the vision of discipleship. As you continue to review the motivating verses in *Friends on the Journey*, the discipling vision will be kept fresh, and you will be encouraged and challenged to continue on this lifelong journey of discipling others.

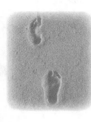

Next Steps on the Journey

Congratulations! You have run a good race and have finished this course of training! As a group, plan a time to celebrate. Be thinking about how your weeks together in *Friends on the Journey* have changed your life so you can share these experiences at your celebration. What are the greatest blessings you received in:

- Your relationship with Jesus?
- Your relationship with others?
- Your friendships in the group?

We, the authors, now draw to a close our part in journeying with you. You are ready to leave the nest and build your own! But be assured that you continue your journey in God's care and in the fellowship of those who have gone before you and will come behind you. The fact that you participated in this discipleship process means you want your life to count for God's kingdom. For that reason, each time we worked on these books, we prayed for you. So we leave you with this encouragement: *"The things you have heard [us] say in the presence of many witnesses, entrust to reliable [women] who will also be qualified to teach others"* (2 Timothy 2:2). And remember, although you may be only one right now, *"the least of you will become a thousand; the smallest a mighty nation!"* (Isaiah 60:22).

Appendix A

MY JOURNEY FRIENDS

Record your group members' names, phone numbers, and e-mail addresses in order to keep in touch with one another. As you grow in relationship with one another, you can also record prayer requests.

Name	Phone	E-mail	Prayer Needs

LEADER'S GUIDELINES

A WOMAN'S JOURNEY OF DISCIPLESHIP is more than a Bible study series. It's a process through which women learn how to walk daily with Jesus and pass on to others that same discipling vision Jesus gave His disciples.

Friends on the Journey seeks to establish God's vision and passion in women for lifelong discipling of others, who in turn will invest their lives in future generations. This study seeks to impart vision, passion, and skills.

Vision: God's Commission to redeem and disciple His women

Passion: God's love expressed to and through His women

Skills: To equip and encourage women to know how to confidently disciple others

Visit www.navigatorchurchministries.org for guidelines to help and inspire you as you step out and lead others through this process of discipleship. On this website, also view the *A Woman's Journey of Discipleship* DVD, and hear stories from women whose hearts have been ignited to follow Jesus Christ and in turn disciple others.

AUTHOR CONTACT INFORMATION

ruthfobes1@verizon.net / Judy Miller: peanutsjam@austin.rr.com

SUGGESTED FORMAT FOR MEETING

- 10 minutes—Casual interaction.
- 35 minutes—Share from your devotional times, review the memory verse, and talk about experiences or new thoughts that were especially encouraging in walking with Jesus during the previous week. Spend a few minutes praying for one another, particularly about personal insights that came as a result of the present week's session.
- 40 minutes—Discuss the session's material, including reflection stories and Travel Guide.
- 5 minutes—End in prayer.

GUIDELINES FOR USING FRIENDS ON THE JOURNEY

- Allow 75-90 minutes for session preparation time, not including My Daily Journey. Encourage group members to spend a little time each day to prepare.
- This study can be used one-to-one or in small groups.
- Sessions can be held weekly or biweekly.

THE LEADER

- The leader should aim to facilitate rather than teach in order to encourage participants to discover truth for themselves.
- We suggest having an assistant leader, who will learn how to lead as she participates with and helps to facilitate a small group.
- The optimum size for small groups is six to eight women. By keeping groups relatively small, each woman is assured of having enough time to be able to share.
- Everyone should be encouraged to use her own journal for My Daily Journey pages, using the model questions provided. This practice is essential for establishing the habit of meeting with the Lord each day.
- At the first meeting, the leader should explain to the group that A WOMAN'S JOURNEY OF DISCIPLESHIP is a process outlined in three books: *Bridges on the Journey*, *Crossroads on the Journey*, and *Friends on the Journey*. These studies can be done separately, but we recommend going through them in sequence. *Bridges* is designed to help women grow from an initial encounter with Jesus into a deeper understanding of how to walk with Him. *Crossroads* encourages women to make choices that will help them walk consistently with Jesus and grow in spiritual maturity and understanding. *Friends* brings them to a deeper relationship that results in learning how to disciple others.
- None of these books guarantees the making of a believer or a disciple. But the process outlined in the books will provide exposure to life with Christ for those who don't know Him yet and will provide opportunities for believers to become established and equipped in spiritual maturity.

- At the first meeting, the leader should explain what to expect on the journey. Here are the chapter components and how to make the most of them:

  - **My Journey Friends.** At your first gathering, encourage your group to record each other's names, phone numbers, and e-mail addresses in appendix A so you can keep in touch with one another. As relationships grow and deepen, you can also record prayer requests for one another.

  - **My Daily Journey.** As the women reflect on what God says to them, explain the importance of using their own journals to record their responses to these two questions: (1) What did I learn about God or myself on my journey? (2) How can I grow deeper in my relationship with the Lord or demonstrate His love to others? For the second question encourage them to respond by writing their thoughts in a prayer. Remember to cover with the group the My Daily Journey explanation, found on page 13 in Session 1. Your group members will be using Acts for their daily devotions. The assignment for each session is listed in Next Steps on the Journey.

  - **Our Journey Together.** This is a time for group members to share recent devotional highlights and lessons learned on their journeys.

  - **Reflections from the Heart of a Discipler.** These are personal stories of different women's journeys with Jesus. Each story relates to the particular topic for the week, giving group members the opportunity to learn from another woman's experience.

  - **The Travel Guide.** The Travel Guide is a Bible study that group members do on their own during the week. As the women explore the Scriptures and learn new truths, they will experience life change. It's important to emphasize that each woman should complete the study before the group meets so she will be ready to share with others during the group time.

  - **Writings on the Way** gives additional perspective from other travelers on their spiritual journeys.

  - **Tips for the Road** is a section that offers practical help and encouragement on your journey of discipleship.

  - **Learning the Route by Heart.** This feature provides group members with a systematic plan for memorizing Scripture, allowing God's Word to be stored in their hearts to transform their thinking and behavior. Bookmarks with each week's memory verse are provided in appendix C. Through consistent review, the women will strengthen this vital habit.

▪ **Next Steps on the Journey.** This is the assignment to be completed before the next meeting.

CELEBRATION

Through God's Holy Spirit and His powerful Word, the women in your group have been transformed from young believers into women ready to disciple others. Wow! What a time to celebrate! We recommend that the leader organize a luncheon or dessert party to celebrate what God has done in the group members' lives. At the end of session 10, set the date and time for this event and invite the women to come with their hearts prepared to share about their journeys with the Lord, to celebrate new and growing relationships with Jesus and new truths learned about following Jesus in discipleship. This is a time for the leaders to affirm and encourage the women in the ways they have seen God transform their lives. It's also a time to challenge the women to continue in a lifelong pattern of investing in future generations through discipleship. Remind them of the personal and individual impact of 2 Timothy 2:2: These things they (the women in your group) have heard (you) say, they (the women in your group) are to entrust to reliable (women) who will be qualified to teach others also.

- Who will they empower with God's vision and passion?
- What spiritual legacy will they leave for the next generation?

ESSENTIALS ON THE JOURNEY

Here are some ideas that we believe are vital to helping women become believers and disciples who follow Jesus all their lives and pass their stories on to others:

- **Small-group relationships.** The focus of your group time should be on developing the women's relationships with Jesus and with each other. Setting an environment of grace and trust allows group members to discover Jesus and be honest in their sharing. Assuring confidentiality is necessary for building trust. This can be instilled in the group by saying simply in each session, "We want each woman to feel comfortable in exploring the Bible and her relationship with Jesus, so please make sure that everything shared in this group stays in this group."

- **Life-to-life.** This means the practice of investing in others from the overflow of your own relationship with Christ. One way you can do this is by sharing personal examples of God's work in changing your life, developing your character, and empowering you for ministry.

- **Spiritual generations.** When God works through one believer to birth a new generation of believers, we call this a "spiritual generation." God's design is for each generation to pass on to others faith lessons and a profound desire to know and obey Him. Each woman can be a link that reaches into the future. It is inspiring to realize that you are not only impacting the individual women in your group but also influencing the new generations they will reach.

- **Discipleship process.** In each session, emphasize that discipleship is a process. By speaking candidly about your personal continuing growth, you will encourage your group to take the next steps on their own journeys and realize that discipleship is a lifelong endeavor.

NOTES

SESSION 1

1. Lee Brase, "Who Me? Make Disciples?" *Discipleship Journal*, November/December 1990, 60.

SESSION 2

1. Dawson Trotman, *Born to Reproduce* (Colorado Springs, CO: NavPress), 9-11, 19-21, 30-31. Dawson Trotman, founder of The Navigators, practiced the principle of spiritual multiplication. He believed that Christians should not just make disciples; they should make disciples who are also disciplemakers. Only then will laborers increase in the unplucked, spiritual harvest.

SESSION 3

1. Lynn Austin, "Mentoring Toward Maturity," *Discipleship Journal*, March/April 1996, 92 (Colorado Springs, CO: NavPress).
2. Becky Brodin, "Finding the Right Person to Disciple," *Discipleship Journal*, January/February 2000, 115 (Colorado Springs, CO: NavPress).

SESSION 4

1. Skip Gray, "Standing On the Promises of God," *Discipleship Journal*, March/April 1982, 8 (Colorado Springs, CO: NavPress). Skip has been a staff member of The Navigators for more than forty years.

SESSION 5

1. Gail MacDonald, *A Step Farther and Higher* (Sisters, OR: Multnomah, 1989), 99-101.

SESSION 6

1. Adapted and used by permission of Michael Dye & Patricia Fancher, The Genesis Process, Genesis Addiction Process and Program, 2004.

2. Arlyn Lawrence, "Restoring Wholeness Through Compassionate Intercession," *Pray! Magazine*, May/June 2007 (Colorado Springs, CO: NavPress).

3. Adapted from the *Healing Prayer* Guidebook, by The Navigators People Resource Team. Used by permission.

SESSION 8

1. Joni Eareckson Tada, "Speaking God's Language," *Discipleship Journal*, May/June 1999, 111 (Colorado Springs, CO: NavPress). Joni is president of JAF Ministries, an organization that accelerates Christian ministry into the disabled community around the world. She is also author of several books, including *When God Weeps* and *More Precious than Silver*.

SESSION 9

1. Mary Zuwerink, *She Shall Flourish: A Tribute to the Power of God in the Life of Beth Mainhood* (self-published, 2005). For more contact information and copies of books: Mary Zuwerink, 3334 Winterbrook Place, Jamestown, NC 27282, (mz@northstate,net).

2. Lorne Sanny, "The Importance of Every Individual," *Discipleship Journal*, March 1981, 2 (Colorado Springs, CO: NavPress). Lorne Sanny was president of The Navigators.

SESSION 10

1. Jennifer Kennedy Dean, *Legacy of Prayer* (Birmingham, AL: New Hope Publishers, 2001), 18.

2. Jim White, "Motivation: For a Lifetime of Disciplemaking," *Discipleship Journal*, May/June 1981, 3 (Colorado Springs, CO: NavPress).

ABOUT THE AUTHORS

GIGI BUSA ministers with Navigator Church Ministries (NCM) of The Navigators, partnering with churches to develop disciplemaking leaders. She served on the pastoral staff at Brookville Baptist Church in Holbrook, Massachusetts. Gigi is a speaker who shares her passion for women to develop a dynamic relationship with Jesus. She and her husband, Buzz, live in Massachusetts and adore being parents and grandparents.

RUTH FOBES and her husband, Bob, partner with pastors and church leaders to develop disciples. They have ministered with The Navigators on college campuses and in communities and neighborhoods and presently serve with Navigator Church Ministries. Ruth's great joy has been to see women whom she has discipled and mentored invest in others. The Fobes live in New England and are blessed to be parents and grandparents.

DIANE MANCHESTER has ministered to women through The Navigators and at Shepherd's Door (a ministry to women and children at Portland Rescue Mission) and has also served on several church pastoral teams. She and her husband, Bruce, live in Portland, Oregon, and have two grown daughters.

NAVIGATOR CHURCH MINISTRIES

NCM focuses on helping churches become more intentional in discipleship and outreach. NCM staff help pastors, church leaders, and lifelong laborers across the United States develop an effective and personalized approach to accomplishing the Great Commission.

NCM works alongside the local church to grow intentional disciplemaking cultures, as reflected in the following illustration:

Growing *intentional* Disciplemaking Cultures
A process to help churches send laborers into their communities

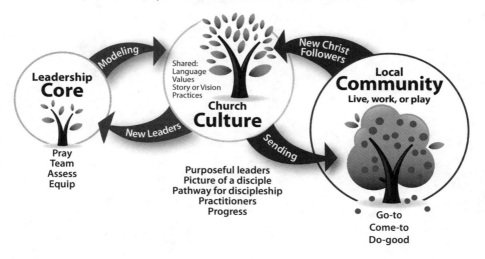

NCM also offers seminars, materials, and coaching to help the local church see discipleship flourish in successive generations. See our web page for further information on how NCM can help you.

www.navigatorchurchministries.org
Call our NCM Office at (719) 594-2446
or write to PO Box 6000, Colorado Springs, CO 80934

Continue on your journey of discipleship.

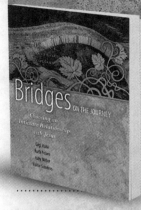

Bridges on the Journey
Ruth Fobes, Gigi Busa, Judy Miller, Vollie Sanders

Bridges on the Journey is a companion to help you and your discipleship group learn the basics of the Christian life — Bible study, living in Christian community, sharing your faith, memorizing Scripture — that will get you started on the right path and keep you going for a lifetime of relationship with Jesus and sharing Him with others.

978-1-60006-786-0

Crossroads on the Journey
Ruth Fobes, Gigi Busa, Diane Manchester, Judy Miller, Vollie Sanders

Crossroads on the Journey takes you deeper in your walk with Jesus, helping you to understand what God has given you through His Word, prayer, and the Holy Spirit to transform your life. Learn what marks a disciple of Jesus, discover your spiritual gifts, and develop the convictions you'll need to persevere in your faith.

978-1-60006-785-3

Friends on the Journey
Ruth Fobes, Gigi Busa, Diane Manchester

Discipleship comes full circle when you pass it on to others in a way that lets them also pass it on. *Friends on the Journey* leads you and your discipleship group into the heart habits, people skills, prayer disciplines, and understandings about God and His passion for the world and love for individuals that will enable you to help women leave behind spiritual generations of people who love Jesus and share Him with others.

978-1-60006-784-6

Available wherever books are sold.   NAVPRESS

Topic: The Great Commission

Then Jesus came to them and said, "All authority in heaven and on earth has been given to me. Therefore go and make disciples of all nations, baptizing them in the name of the Father and of the Son and of the Holy Spirit, and teaching them to obey everything I have commanded you. And surely I am with you always, to the very end of the age."

(MATTHEW 28:18-20)

Topic: Ministering Life-to-Life

We were gentle among you, like a mother caring for her little children. We loved you so much that we were delighted to share with you not only the gospel of God but our lives as well, because you had become so dear to us.

(1 THESSALONIANS 2:7-8)

Topic: God's Promises and Power

I thank my God every time I remember you. In all my prayers for all of you, I always pray with joy.

(PHILIPPIANS 1:3-4)

Topic: Spiritual Discipline

Train yourself to be godly. For physical training is of some value, but godliness has value for all things, holding promise for both the present life and the life to come.

(1 TIMOTHY 4:7-8)

Topic: Healing and Transformation

The Spirit of the Sovereign LORD is on me, because the LORD has anointed me to preach good news to the poor. He has sent me to bind up the brokenhearted, to proclaim freedom for the captives and release from darkness for the prisoners.

(ISAIAH 61:1)

Topic: Relationship with Jesus

We proclaim him, admonishing and teaching everyone with all wisdom, so that we may present everyone perfect in Christ. To this end I labor, struggling with all his energy, which so powerfully works in me.

(COLOSSIANS 1:28-29)

Topic: The Importance of the Word

All Scripture is God-breathed and is useful for teaching, rebuking, correcting and training in righteousness, so that the man of God may be thoroughly equipped for every good work.

(2 TIMOTHY 3:16-17)

Topic: The Value of Each Individual

The least of you will become a thousand, the smallest a mighty nation. I am the LORD; in its time I will do this swiftly.

(ISAIAH 60:22)

Topic: Spiritual Generations

And the things you have heard me say in the presence of many witnesses entrust to reliable men who will also be qualified to teach others.

(2 TIMOTHY 2:2)